Faith
is a Journey

by

Father John

Grosvenor House
Publishing Limited

All rights reserved
Copyright © Father John, 2021

The right of Father John to be identified as the author of this
work has been asserted in accordance with Section 78
of the Copyright, Designs and Patents Act 1988

The book cover picture is copyright to Isabelle Sigournay

This book is published by
Grosvenor House Publishing Ltd
Link House
140 The Broadway, Tolworth, Surrey, KT6 7HT.
www.grosvenorhousepublishing.co.uk

This book is sold subject to the conditions that it shall not, by way of
trade or otherwise, be lent, resold, hired out or otherwise circulated
without the author's or publisher's prior consent in any form of binding or
cover other than that in which it is published and
without a similar condition including this condition being imposed
on the subsequent purchaser.

A CIP record for this book
is available from the British Library

ISBN 978-1-83975-597-2

Jesus answered, 'I was born for this, I came
Into the world for this, to bear witness to the
truth; and all who are on the side of truth
listen to my voice.'
'Truth?' said Pilate. 'What is that?'
(Jn 18 : 37-38)

Religion is the search to know, and the response to what we discover about the Supreme Being (the Ultimate Truth) in whom we live and move and have our being.

Because it demands a personal response, religion can be a very upsetting thing, involving sudden or gradual change in attitude towards people and things, requiring decisions about life-style and the rearranging of priorities.

This is what we call conversion.

Without the latter, religion is just the means to achieving a personal ambition.

This is what gives religion a bad name.

*After 35 years as a missionary in Africa
and 20 years as a Parish Priest in England,
Father John shares his thoughts and observations.
Refreshing. Inspiring. Uplifting.*

2nd Sunday of Advent (C) 2015

Jesus of Nazareth came to proclaim the Kingdom of God.

The Kingdom of God is mentioned about 70 times in the New Testament.

Jesus of Nazareth did not come just to proclaim the Kingdom of God but also to actually initiate it and to set it up as an existing and running entity.

How did this happen?

He started with repentance.

If we want to have a good relationship with anyone we must first repent and apologise for any hurt or harm we have done to them.

The ministry of Jesus of Nazareth began with his Baptism by John in the Jordan. This Baptism was a sign of true repentance and reconciliation.

John proclaimed him as the one who was to come - the one for whom he was preparing the way. Thus many of John's disciples became followers of Jesus.

From these followers Jesus picked twelve persons whom he called apostles. These were called, and required, to leave everything and be his constant companions as he travelled the roads and pathways of Galilee, preaching about, proclaiming and living the Kingdom or Reign of God.

This was the inner core. Then there were the other 72 disciples who, though not required to leave everything and be his constant companions, were around a lot of the time and were also sent ahead of him to prepare the people for his later arrival in their villages. These 72 spent a share of time, off and on, with the core group but had also to go home frequently to look after their families and home affairs generally.

Then there were those (who were very many) who joined the group for a day or two to hear the 'Good News' from Jesus. These had to return home permanently after a day or two or three, but were instrumental in spreading the news about Jesus far and wide.

Then there were those who, though not part of the group, but had met, heard and believed in Jesus, who always opened their homes to Jesus and the apostles whenever they were nearby. They provided them with food and lodging for as long as they needed. (People like Martha, Mary and Lazarus).

Then there were those who were happy to give them something to eat if they were passing nearby. Then there were those who were curious about Jesus, not sure what to make of the whole thing but not hostile.

This motley group of people, centred on Jesus of Nazareth, living, to a greater or lesser degree, in union with his teaching and example, were the embodiment of what Jesus called the 'kingdom of god.'- 'the reign of God.' They tried to live in a 'Godly' way, therefore God reigned among them.

When asked by the Pharisees about the Kingdom of God, Jesus replied 'the kingdom of God is among you.'

Jesus spoke of the kingdom of God not as something in the unspecified future.

He spoke of the kingdom as having already been initiated, as something existing now. For us of our parish today, the kingdom of God is among us when our parish, or a group of parishioners, get together to do something. For example, a group met as the parish pastoral council last Thursday evening. They worked without pay. They give of their time, expertise or money with no visible reward. This self - giving, this co - operation, for the common good, is the kingdom of God.

The same is true of any group of parishioners getting together and cooperating.

Just as, in the group of Jesus and his followers, each called differently, to participate in sundry ways, was the kingdom of God at that time in Galilee, so too our parish, united around Jesus our leader, each participating in different ways and to differing degrees, is the kingdom of god here today.

As in Jesus of Nazareth's day, differences of opinion occur within the Kingdom. This is normal and even healthy as long as differing opinions are not immovable and compromise and mutual accommodation is achieved.

The I/Thou relationship with God has its place but it must be within the we/Thou relationship of the Kingdom of God.

3rd Sunday of Advent (C) 2015

'And the crowds asked John, 'What then should we do?" In reply he said to them, 'Whoever has two coats must share with anyone who has none; and whoever has food must do likewise.

That is Christianity. That is the Kingdom of God. That is the reign of God.

We have turned Christianity into a comfortable bourgeoisie way of life. We have turned our church into a middleclass country club.

Looking at us, who would guess that our founder was executed on a cross, by the government and religious leaders of his day, as a dangerous subversive,

Our church, the way I and you live our faith, instead of having the power to transform an affluent, self-centred society, is enslaved and sucked dry by this very society which we were meant to transform.

I know that as a parish we do much to promote the Kingdom of God. I know we do much to help the needy. I know that Pope Francis is doing much to sensitise our Church to the plight of the poor and the suffering.

But we are still, in the eyes of much of humanity, a well off, middleclass, organisation.

As Jesus suggests in Lk. 17; When you have done all that you were ordered to do, say, 'We are worthless slaves; we have done only what we ought to have done!'

There are still many who do not have a coat while our

closets are overflowing. There are still many with no bread while our fridges are stuffed full.

I must not shrug off my duty and responsibility by saying 'I have done my bit.'

A quick examination of my closet and fridge will convince me that I can do much more. As a Christian I will never reach the stage where I can say 'I have done my bit.'

After all I have not yet been hung up on a cross to die.

Sometimes, someone would ask me to pray for the victims of some major disaster during the 'prayer of the faithful.' You may have noticed that I do not do so.

The reason is that I am too embarrassed to ask God to help them, while I myself am sitting on resources that could help, and have not done so, or have only contributed a small amount. Or do I want God to point this out to me?

Why on earth do we continually ask our God to help the needy when He has already supplied us with everything that is needed?

There is something here for me to think about this Advent.

4TH SUNDAY OF ADVENT (C)
2015

Imagine yourself living around the beginning of the first millennium AD. About 2015 years ago. Your parents are thrifty and own a few acres of land and a few goats and sheep. You are related, in one way or another, to many of the other residents of Nazareth and help each other out when the need arises. You are a young girl of about 15 years old and promised in marriage to a local carpenter named Joseph who was twice your age. Up to this point everything is normal for that time and place. There are no problems.

Then one day you are weaving at home or perhaps out gathering firewood when something strange and unsettling happens. You become aware of some presence, startling, but not threatening or frightening. Thinking back on it afterwards you find it hard to put the whole affair into words but you distinctly remember being offered a great gift, without much explanation or guidance, and accepting it at face value.

This gift you were offered was something which every young girl in Israel dreamed and fantasised about - the great honour of being chosen as the mother of the long awaited Redeemer.

All excited, you ran to your mum and blurted out that you were chosen by God to be the mother of the redeemer. Your mother, used to such girlish notions, told you to stop daydreaming and to get on with your household chores. Somewhat deflated you told your dad who just gave you a hug and laughed heartily.

You confided in your best friend who listened attentively and then told you she was going to be the mother of the next Roman Emperor.

So what to do?

You kept quiet and got on with your daily chores.

That was fine until there were more changes. You became aware that your body was changing. Then the enormity of what was happening began to dawn on you. You were pregnant, were not yet married and the punishment for adulterous women was stoning to death. You panicked. You cried out to God. Nothing happened. You eventually calmed down and began to think.

You had heard the news about Zachariah the priest, who was related to you, and how he had seen a vision in the temple, telling him that his wife Elizabeth would have a son, although she was well past childbearing age. You knew that your parents would go ballistic if you told them you were pregnant. So you decided that you must visit Elisabeth who might listen to you and believe you. Telling your parents that Elizabeth would need someone to help her at this time you hurried off on the long journey to Elizabeth's place.

Today's Gospel reading tells the rest of the story. Elisabeth believed her. Zachariah, after his recent experience in the temple, believed her. When John the Baptist was born Mary returned home. I presume Zachariah went with her. Had a long talk with her parents and later with Joseph. As a priest of the Temple he would be believed and have great influence with them.

Mary got a great gift from God. Every gift has to be lived with. Every gift has its problems. Mary had to use her own common sense and ingenuity to solve these problems. A call to marriage is a great gift from God. A call to priesthood is a great gift from God. A call to parenthood is a great gift from God. Each gift brings its problems which have to be solved with one's own common sense and ingenuity. These latter are also God's gifts.

Christmas (C) 2015

What an amazing thing Christmas is for us.

We all groan (at least the adults do) at the thought of the stress and bustle of Christmas but we wouldn't be without it for the world.

It brings out the best in us. We remember, and buy gifts for, people we would normally not think about. Above all it unites families. Even family members who are scattered throughout the world try and get together for Christmas.

In Africa the cities and towns become ghost towns at Christmas. Everybody goes back to their home place for the week of Christmas.

Christmas is all about family, and reconnecting at our deepest roots.

Despite the commercial juggernaut that Christmas has become it is still centred on family unity.

We have all seen people in serious trouble going to or leaving court. No matter what bad things they have done, or are accused of doing, they are almost always accompanied by a family member or members. This is as it should be. Our family is our support in all circumstances. How sad it is to see someone in trouble only accompanied and supported by a lawyer.

Of course there are people who for one reason or another do not have family. Could we consider including them in our family Christmas?

The centrepiece of our Christmas is the crib. As you can see, it is a family. Dad, Mum and child. What a great idea God had when he chose the family as his entry point into our lives. Most of us would willingly die to save our child. Many would willingly die to save any child. When I think of God I think of Him/Her as a parent. I am God's child.

What is wrong with thinking of God as my child, especially at Christmas?

And what would I not do for my child?

Epiphany (C) 2016

Epiphany is a showing, a demonstrating, a revealing.

Today - the feast of the Epiphany - remembers and celebrates the fact that Christianity is not just for the People of Israel but is for all peoples.

(During the first century AD this latter point was the source of much dispute and contention among Christians of Jewish origin).

We often hear a person comment on the impression they received when visiting a particular church or congregation. I felt welcome. I felt at home. I felt excluded. I felt unwelcome. I felt I was intruding. I felt I was being judged.

Each one of us is an Epiphany. You and I, by our actions and attitude, reveal to others what our Church is like, what our God is like.

I may think that how I act or conduct myself in Church is my business. Nothing could be further from the truth. I have heard people state that because of something I, or another member of the congregation, said or did, they will not be back.

The opposite is also true. Many are attracted and convinced not by erudite sermons but by how they were treated when they did come.

So Epiphany is not something that happened 2000 years ago and which we celebrate and remember. It is something which I must be, in and about the Church. It is something I must be at work. It is something I must be for my marriage partner, for my children, for my friends, for my parents.

This is basic and fundamental evangelising.

This is something we can all do.

Every night before retiring it is a good idea to examine my day. I must ask myself; was I an epiphany of my God to the people I met today?

Baptism of the Lord (C) 2016

There are three words used by world religions which are widely misused and misunderstood by the users.

They are 'Fear of the Lord,' Judgment" and 'Atonement.'

World religions use 'Fear of the Lord' in the sense of being afraid of a ruler or tyrant who is liable to incarcerate and torture you if displeased.

World religions use the word 'Judgment' as in a court of law where one is accused of misdeeds, found guilty and sentenced to punishment.

World religions use the word 'Atonement' as in the service or action by which a debt is paid. Or by the punishment imposed in retribution for a crime committed.

That is how these three words (or phrases) are used and understood today.

This is not what Scripture means by these words. This is not what God means by these words in the Bible.

In the Bible 'Fear of the Lord' is used in the sense of the reluctance or unwillingness of a well loved child to do anything that might embarrass or inconvenience or discomfit or hurt a dearly loved parent. The idea of subsequent punishment does not enter into the meaning. In the Bible 'Judgment' is used in the sense of fair distribution, equal sharing, alleviation of oppression, each person getting their fair slice of the cake. The idea of judgment as a declaration of innocence or guilt followed by release or punishment, is not relevant or envisioned.

In the Bible the word 'Atonement' has nothing to do with anything I (a human being) have to do or suffer so as to pay off a debt.

In the Biblical sense 'atonement' is initiated by God and proceeds from God. It is the gift from God of being enabled to live in God's presence - in God's 'space'- despite my unholiness and constantly recurring guilt.

Atonement in the Bible is akin to reconciliation but not exactly similar. Reconciliation involves movement on the part of two persons. Each has a part to play in becoming reconciled. Atonement is a unilateral movement. It is God who does the atoning.

Remember the story of the prodigal son. It is the father who runs to welcome him. It is the father who takes him in his arms. It is the father who reinstalls him as his son with full rights and privileges. It is the father who brushes aside and refuses to listen to his son's excuses, explanations, and efforts at atonement.

So where does the prodigal son come into all this? Where do I come into all this? I and the prodigal son are always free to walk away from God.

But the natural, human response is one of gratitude.

With a heart overflowing with gratitude I determine to, at all times, seek to do the will of my God.

In our understanding of 'atonement' it is impossible for a human being, no matter what they do, to atone to the Infinite God in any meaningful way. It is only God who can do the atoning (in the Bible's understanding of the word).

1 Jn 4:8 'God's love was revealed among us in this way .. that he sent his Son to be the atoning sacrifice for our sins.' And again 'If anyone does sin, we have an advocate with the Father, Jesus Christ the righteous; and he is the atoning sacrifice for our sins.'

The above calls into question the whole idea and practice of my atoning to God for my sins or for the sins of others (as in the allegedly suffering souls in Purgatory).

2ND SUNDAY OF THE YEAR (C) 2016

In today's Gospel reading we see something about Jesus of Nazareth which is generally ignored.

He didn't just supply a certain quantity of wine. He supplied 150 gallons of first class wine. This was not just sufficient but an abundance.

When he fed the 500 there was not just sufficient, but an abundance - 12 baskets full left over.

When he fed the four thousand there was again an abundance - seven baskets full left over. 'A great crowd of his disciples and a large number of the people from all Judea and Jerusalem and the coastal region of Tyre and Sidon came to hear him and to be healed of their diseases; and even those who were tormented by unclean spirits were cured. Everyone in the crowd sought to touch him because power came forth from him and healed them all.' Again an abundance of healing.

Jesus of Nazareth enjoyed life and companionship as much as possible. 'Now John's disciples and the Pharisees were fasting; and people came and said to him, 'Why do John's disciples and the disciples of the Pharisees fast, but your disciples do not fast?'

Then they said to him, "John's disciples, like the disciples of the Pharisees, frequently fast and pray, but your disciples eat and drink.'

'John the Baptist came neither eating food nor drinking wine, and you said, 'He is possessed by a demon.' The Son of

Man came eating and drinking and you said, 'Look, he is a glutton and a drunkard, a friend of tax collectors and sinners.'

It is amazing how often we read in the Gospels where Jesus was at table when he made some point or taught a lesson. He often spoke of the Kingdom of God as reclining at table and being served an abundance of rich food and drink.

In his parable about God's forgiveness we have the father going completely overboard in welcoming the prodigal son back home. Nothing was spared. Nothing was too much. Everything, including forgiveness and welcome, was in abundance, 'overflowing, pressed down, shaken together and running over.'

In the life of Jesus of Nazareth everything was in the superlative, everything in abundance. Was his death not an abundance of pain and sorrow? Was his resurrection not an abundance of joy and hope.

Is this not something admirable, something well worth aiming at in my life. Is this not the Reign of God, the Kingdom of God. How can I be mean and small minded if my life is a walk with Jesus of Nazareth?

If I claim to live in the presence of my God, how can I collect and hoard more than my fair share of the abundance of this world, while others are in serious need?

3rd Sunday of the Year (C) 2016

"The Spirit of the Lord is upon me, because he has anointed me to bring good news to the poor. He has sent me to proclaim release to the captives and recovery of sight to the blind, to let the oppressed go free, to proclaim the year of the Lord's favour."

In a nutshell the above quotation is the reason why Jesus of Nazareth (God made man) was born, lived and died among us and was raised from the dead.

The above is how our God wants us to live.

The above is how our God wants world affairs - political, economic and religious - to be run. The above is not meant as something to be hoped for in the distant future. It is something our God wants for us here and now.

It is how my God wants me to conduct my affairs, to live my life today.

Bringing good news to the poor is not just assuring them that God loves them, but proving it by doing all in my power to alleviate their poverty, here and now, in a practical way.

The biggest problem for people in Galilee in Jesus' time was nomadic landless people who had been forced into migrant labour by unjust taxation which forced them to borrow, with their piece of land as collateral, which was then seized when they defaulted on the debt. The rich grew richer and the poor grew poorer (a familiar condition today). Many ended up in jail for non-payment of debts.

So when Jesus spoke of release of captives and the oppressed going free these were the people who immediately came to mind.

The 'year of the Lord's favour' was called a' Jubilee Year' in the Old Testament.

This meant that every fifty years debts should be cancelled and land, forfeited due to inability to repay debts, should be returned to its original owner. This is what God wanted the Israelites to practise but of course they never did.

Recovery of sight to the blind indicates God's desire of healing for all humankind.

Jesus of Nazareth not only brought us this Good News but lived it in every detail throughout his life. As we read in Acts. "He went about doing good and healing all those oppressed by the devil, for God was with him." This is authentic Christianity.

Everything else to do with the Christian Religion is secondary.

Without this basic focus in our lives towards mercy, compassion, forgiveness, fair dealing, justice, sharing, love etc. the outward trappings of Christianity are just that - outward trappings. Their function is to keep me constantly focused on the essentials of Christianity and help me to live by them - to help me to walk in the footsteps of Jesus of Nazareth.

Will I ever succeed in living every day of my life as a true Christian?

The answer is no.

But realising my shortcomings is very good for me.

It is called humility.

4th Sunday of the Year (C) 2016

Today's Gospel reading is a continuation of last Sunday's reading.

Last Sunday we saw Jesus of Nazareth visiting his home village of Nazareth for the first time after he started his ministry. He presented himself and his way of life as the fulfillment of the passage in the book of Isaiah. He spoke well and all were impressed and welcoming. In today's reading the mood abruptly changes. It becomes hostile. So hostile in fact that they want to kill him.

Some scripture scholars postulate two separate visits to Nazareth. The first one Jesus presented himself as the fulfillment of the prophesy of the Old Testament. The bringer of the Good News from God. The initiator of the Reign or Kingdom of God.

The second visit Jesus gets down to what the above means for the everyday lives of the people of Nazareth. He points out how, even in the small backward village of Nazareth, there is oppression and injustice. Many Nazarenes do not like this. They do not like their lifestyle to be criticized, their faults highlighted.

They react angrily. So much so that they want to get rid of him permanently. Luke may have telescoped these two visits into one for the following reason.

This response of some of the citizens of Nazareth - those responsible for injustices and oppression of the poor and needy - mirrors and forecasts the same kind of response which came later from the leaders of Israel, both secular and religious, in Jerusalem, which culminated in his execution on a cross. The official rejection of God's Redeemer by the people of Israel.

It is sobering for me to contemplate that if I really walked in the footsteps of Jesus of Nazareth I too would sometimes get the same response.

As Jesus promised his followers "See, I am sending you out like sheep into the midst of wolves; so be wise as serpents and innocent as doves. Beware of them, for they will hand you over to councils and flog you in their synagogues; and you will be dragged before governors and kings because of me."

So as a serious Christian I can expect welcome and respect, but also, from those whose lifestyle I challenge, hostility and abuse.

So, perhaps, if sometimes you angrily hustle me out of your church and tell me to go back to where I came from, it may only indicate that I am on the right track ! !

5th Sunday of the Year (C) 2016

Peter fell down at Jesus' knees, saying, "Go away from me, Lord, for I am a sinful man!" Jesus said to Simon, "Do not be afraid; from now on you will be catching men."

For Peter to qualify as the rock on which Jesus built his church; for Peter to qualify as the leader of the Apostles; it was essential that he wholeheartedly believe, accept and acknowledge, even openly, that he was a sinful man.

This is what qualified him to be an Apostle, that qualified him to be the leader of Christ's church.

If we think back on recent church scandals it is obvious that our church was severely damaged by the scandals themselves, but far more so by the cover-up; the refusal to admit culpability. The refusal to acknowledge that we are a church of sinners, from top to bottom. We forgot or ignored the words of Jesus of Nazareth our founder;

'I desire mercy, not sacrifice. I did not come to call the righteous but sinners.'

And again; 'Some scribes who were Pharisees .... said to his disciples, "Why does he eat with tax collectors and sinners?" Jesus heard this and said to them, 'Those who are well do not need a physician, but the sick do. I did not come to call the righteous but sinners.'

And again; 'If we say that we have no sin, we deceive ourselves, and the truth is not in us. If we say that we have not sinned, we make him a liar, and his word is not in us.'

This is what Pope Francis is trying to do - to change us from being a church of Pharisees into a church of sinners.

Of course the very same applies to I myself. I 'oh and ah' about the faults of others while keeping my own hidden away at the back of the cupboard. I delight to hear of the sins of others but get very annoyed and in a huff when my own are mentioned.

This does not mean I go around revealing my sins to all and sundry - this can be just another form of pride. What is needed is a constant forgiving, accepting and compassionate attitude of mind. A total belief and understanding that we are all up to our knees in the same stable.

1st Sunday of Lent (c) 2016

The temptations of Jesus: These are temptations which Jesus of Nazareth had to cope with and struggle against all his life. They are not 'once off' things.

They are presented in today's reading in a stylized way.

These temptations are also presented as a warning or as a commentary on the temptations which confront the followers of Jesus as an organisation (The Church) and as individuals. They are true for all time and are true for me today.

The first temptation is to self interest. Which of us can truthfully say, I am not motivated by self interest in what I do, at least to some extent?'

The most famous one is 'it is in our national interest.'

Or 'we must protect the good name of our church.'

The second temptation is to seek power, control, authority. Particularly susceptible to this temptation are the clergy. Personally I have difficulties with massive liturgical events with multitudes of church dignitaries decked out in fantastic medieval fancy dress and cheered on by thousands of sycophantic and adoring followers. I cannot see it as something which Jesus of Nazareth would associate himself with. Many would not agree with me on this.

This temptation to power and control can also exist within my family.

The third temptation is to personal ostentation and self-display. To use God, to use the Church and the space provided by the Church, to seek reputation, prestige and honour. How does this fit in with Jesus of Nazareth who said 'who is greater, the one who is at the table or the one who serves? Is it not the one at the table? But I am among you as one who serves.'

The temptation of Jesus of Nazareth must be understood in the context of place and time. He became incredibly famous in a very short time. God had granted Him great power and ability. Vast crowds came to him, listened to him and followed him all over Galilee. People had great expectations of him as a possible Messiah, as a possible King, as a great revolutionary leader who would defeat the Romans and set up a new kingdom of Israel. The temptation to go along with these expectations must have been great.

As we see on Palm Sunday this temptation was being aggressively pushed on him right up to the end.

It is obvious that the New Testament sees selfishness, hunger for power and using God and the Church for self aggrandisement as the greatest temptations that Jesus of Nazareth had to contend with.

Is not the same true for the Church today?

And what if that person is also my God and my Creator?

2nd Sunday of Lent (C) 2016

Today's Gospel reading has many layers of meaning. Here are some.

1) It is a lesson for Christ's followers of that time.

The Apostles, disciples and followers of Jesus of Nazareth were of many minds as to who and what Jesus was. Was he a new prophet, or Elijah risen from the dead, or John the Baptist risen from the dead etc. or as his relatives believed, someone who had lost his mind. Today's Gospel reveals to Peter, James & John something of what Jesus really was.

While they were praying the three apostles dozed off and suddenly awakening they see Jesus 'in his glory.' They are startled and fearful. Seeing Jesus conversing with Moses and Elijah, Peter takes Jesus as being of huge importance - the equal of Moses, the Lawgiver and Elijah, the greatest of the Prophets.

But he is immediately corrected. A voice from the cloud (the voice of God) tells him that Jesus of Nazareth is far more than a Moses or an Elijah. He is the Son of God and from now on it is He, not Moses or Elijah, who must be listened to and followed.

2) It is a lesson for me today.

I too underestimate the importance of people just as his apostles underestimated the importance and true nature of Jesus of Nazareth. I look at, and am influenced by, the accidents of a person rather than realising their true worth.

Accidents is a philosophical term describing the non essential properties of a person or thing. Accidents are size, shape, taste, smell, weight, features, colour, accent, education, etc. All these are non essential and variable.

Then there is the substance. In philosophy substance is what makes something to be what it is. For example in the Eucharist the substance of bread and wine are changed into the Body and Blood of Jesus Christ. The accidents - colour, taste, shape etc. - remain the same.

The lesson for me today is to avoid falling into the same error as regards the people I know and meet as the apostles did with Jesus of Nazareth.

I judge people on the accidents when I should look beyond the accidents to the substance of the person.

(For example one can look on the accidents only and regard the Eucharist as just another piece of white bread. Or one can see deeper with the eyes of faith and see the substance -the real presence of Jesus of Nazareth.)

In other words I must look on others with the eyes of God their Creator. I must look beyond the accidents and see them in their true glory as children of God.

Something else to occupy my time with during this Lent.

3rd Sunday of Lent (C) 2016

At the present time a hotly debated subject in theology is judgment, punishment, atonement, reparation.

In the old days this whole thing was simple; Man, by Original Sin, totally disrupted God's plans for creation. This landed human beings in the mess we find ourselves in and also annoyed God no end. The results were death, suffering, grief, sickness, earthquakes, tsunamis, volcanic eruptions, hurricanes, crime etc. etc.

God the Son, the Second Person of the Holy Trinity, became a human being and sacrificed himself on a cross, so that He could atone to God the Father for the insult inflicted on him by ungrateful human beings.

This was a nice simple, 'catch all' explanation, totally adequate for simple, uneducated people especially as no better explanation existed at the time.

Today this is inadequate, simplistic and untrue.

Puny man cannot, and never will, disrupt God's plan for creation.

We see in the first part of today's Gospel reading how the people of Jesus' day believed all this. All suffering, accidents, and disasters were the direct result of sinning and demonstrated God's punishment for people who sinned. It was God's judgment on sinners.

Jesus was adamant that this was not true. 'I tell you, no!' was his reply.

Then he goes on to explain what he meant by judgment.

Judgment for Jesus of Nazareth was my decision, my responsibility.

Jesus came to Bring the 'Good News.' I am free to accept it or reject it. I am free to be of service to others or to serve only my own interests. My decision is Judgment.

Like the fig tree I am encouraged to make the right judgment, I am helped to make the right judgment, I am given time to make the right judgment. The buck stops with me. It is my judgment or decision.

Jesus informs us, warns us, about the results of making the wrong decision, the wrong judgment. It is not an irate God who will bring disaster. It is the consequences of my own wrong judgment, of my own wrong decision, which visit me with disaster.

If I look back on my life, carefully and truthfully, I can see this.

When I judge or decide on the basis of self-interest the consequences of this wrong judgment can be seen not only in my own life but also in international and world affairs. Judgments made with self-interested as motivation - the famous 'in our own national interest' -will always come back to bite one. The chickens will eventually come home to roost.

This is the judgment I should worry about.

Easter Sunday (C) 2016

The four accounts of the Resurrection as we read in the four Gospels make interesting reading.

Mtt. This was Mary Magdalene and the other Mary; 'So they left the tomb quickly with fear and great joy, and ran to tell his disciples. Suddenly Jesus met them and said, "Greetings!" And they came to him, took hold of his feet, and worshiped him. Then Jesus said to them, "Do not be afraid; go and tell my brothers to go to Galilee; there they will see me."

Mark. This was Mary of Magdala; 'Now after he rose early on the first day of the week, he appeared first to Mary Magdalene, from whom he had cast out seven demons. She went out and told those who had been with him, while they were mourning and weeping. But when they heard that he was alive and had been seen by her, they would not believe it.'

Luke. This was Mary of Magdala, Joanna and Mary the mother of James; An angel appeared to them at the tomb and told them that He had risen. They ran back to the Apostles etc. with their news - 'but this story of theirs seemed pure nonsense, and they did not believe them.'

John. 'Mary stood weeping outside the tomb. As she wept, she bent over to look into the tomb; and she saw two angels in white, sitting where the body of Jesus had been lying, one at the head and the other at the feet. They said to her, "Woman, why are you weeping?' She said to them, "They have taken away my Lord, and I do not know where they have laid him." When she had said this, she turned around and saw Jesus standing there, but she did not know that it was Jesus. Jesus said to her, 'Woman, why are you weeping? Whom are you looking for?' Supposing him to be the gardener, she said to him, "Sir, if you have carried him away, tell me where you have laid him, and I will take him away." Jesus said to her, "Mary!" She turned and said to him in Hebrew, "Rabbouni!" (which means Teacher).

Is this not convincing evidence that the first to witness the Risen Lord were these loyal female disciples of Jesus? These did not abandon him. These followed him all the way to Calvary and did not run away and hide.

Yet these obvious facts seem to have been 'slid over.' We have St. Paul who did not become a Christian until years later, stating officially the doctrine he had been handed on by Peter (Cephas) and the Apostles was as follower; 'For I handed on to you as of first importance what I in turn had received: that Christ died for our sins in accordance with the scriptures, and that he was buried, and that he was raised on the third day in accordance with the scriptures, and that he appeared to Cephas, then to the twelve. Then he appeared to more than five hundred brothers and sisters at one time, most of whom are still alive, though some have died. Then he appeared to James, then to all the apostles. Last of all, as to one untimely born, he appeared also to me. Obviously some sleight of hand has occurred. People who were obviously the first witnesses to the Resurrection in all the Gospel accounts have been quietly relegated to the position of indefinite third-fourth divisions. This happened a long time ago but is still happening today!! Unless our church ladies grasp their heritage, acknowledge it as true and implement it fearlessly, things will remain as they are for the next 2000 years.

3rd Sunday of Easter (C) 2016

Today's Gospel reading is loaded with Christian theology, illustrated by symbols.

Although the historical accuracy of the event is largely irrelevant that does not mean that it was not an actual event.

The disciples on their own initiative decide to go fishing (the first symbol is that their initiative does not involve the Risen Lord).

They fish all night (without the involvement of the Risen Lord they are in the dark). They catch nothing (again without Jesus' involvement and help they achieve nothing).

They emerge from the darkness, tired and depressed, into the light of day and discern somebody standing on the shore and calling to them. Although they do not immediately recognise him they follow his instructions and catch a huge haul of fish.

Their eyes are opened and they recognise him.

Jesus' first concern is for the disciples' total wellbeing - they are spiritually and mentally uplifted by what happened and by the presence of the Risen Lord but they are also physically tired and hungry. So the first thing Jesus wants for them is to sit down and have a hearty breakfast which he has prepared for them and serves to them. (Echoes of his words to them -'here am I among you as one who serves.')

This has been a salutary lesson for the disciples and especially for Peter.

Since Peter has emerged as an acknowledged leader among the disciples, and tends to be overly self-reliant on, and confidant in, his own strength and ability, Jesus presses ahead with the lesson on the necessity for the involvement of the Risen Lord in all their deliberations and initiatives and the constant need for his guidance and strength if their work is to bear fruit.

So he asks Peter the question 'do you love me more than these' three times. This graphically reminds Peter of his boastful declaration on the way to Jerusalem, "Master I will lay down my life for you" yet when the crunch comes he fearfully denies even knowing Jesus.

Only when this lesson has been truly learned and accepted, does Jesus accept Peter into the leadership role.

The lesson for us today is that, as a parish, we will always bear fruit as long as what we decide to do, or be, is decided under the guidance of and with total confidence in the help and support of the Risen Lord.

Every decision we make must be decided together in the presence of Jesus of Nazareth.

4th Sunday of Easter (C) 2016

You are all well aware of how confusing and frustrating it is to try and get your head around the terms and conditions of say a credit card, an insurance policy, a contract of sale, tax returns etc. etc. After reading pages and pages of small print one abandons the effort in angry frustration. Obfuscation seems to be an essential ingredient in the makeup of the human psyche. (Witness the present 'debate' about 'in' or 'out.')

Understandably, but unfortunately, it is also present in the practice of religion. Most of us 'cannot see the wood for the trees.'

Jesus of Nazareth didn't obfuscate. For example take today's Gospel reading: 'My sheep listen to my voice and they follow me.'

So what does his voice say? - what does Jesus of Nazareth tell us?

Let theologians and philosophers of sundry persuasions ask this question and we end up as confused as we are presently with the 'in'- 'out' debate.

So let's stick to His own words.

"I give you a new commandment, that you love one another. Just as I have loved you, you also should love one another. By this everyone will know that you are my disciples, if you have love for one another."

This is great, it is very clear.

But some might ask; Does this mean that we must all fall on each other's necks and become lovey-dovey, or what?

Jesus of Nazareth, again, gives us a very straight and understandable answer.

"Do not judge, and you will not be judged; do not condemn, and you will not be condemned. Forgive, and you will be forgiven; give, and it will be given to you. A good measure, pressed down, shaken together, running over, will be put into your lap; for the measure you give will be the measure you get back."

That is how I follow Jesus of Nazareth.

This is basic Christianity. Every other religious practice or devotion is to remind us of this, and to help us to do it. If it doesn't do this for me it is a waste of my time and energy.

5th Sunday of Easter (C) 2016

We read last week; 'My sheep listen to my voice ... and they follow me.'

We saw, in Jesus' own words, what following Jesus means. In today's Gospel we are told 'love one another as I have loved you.'

Let's see what He meant by 'as I have loved you.' What did he do to show his love. Jesus again gives me another simple lesson on what exactly he means.

"The kings of the Gentiles lord it over them; and those in authority over them are called benefactors. But not so with you; rather the greatest among you must become like the youngest, and the leader like one who serves. For who is greater, the one who is at the table or the one who serves? Is it not the one at the table? But I am among you as one who serves."

And again; "After he had washed their feet, had put on his robe, and had returned to the table, he said to them, "Do you know what I have done to you? You call me Teacher and Lord —and you are right, for that is what I am. So if I, your Lord and Teacher, have washed your feet, you also ought to wash one another's feet. For I have set you an example, that you also should do as I have done to you."

And again as we saw in the Gospel reading a couple of weeks ago; The disciples had spent the whole night fishing and caught nothing. When they had gone ashore, they saw a charcoal fire there, with fish on it, and bread. 'Jesus said to them, "Come and have breakfast." .... 'Jesus came and took the bread and gave it to them, and did the same with the fish.'

Let's analyse this a bit. Jesus had to get charcoal, he had to bring it to the lakeside, he had to light the charcoal. He had to get some fish and bread, he had to pick some flat stones on which to cook the food over the fire, he had to attend to the fire and the food as it cooked, he had to share it out among the disciples, he had to tidy up afterwards.

This is nothing extraordinary. Parents do it for their family all the time. But as we all know being of service to ones family is one thing, being equally of service to those outside ones immediate family is quite another thing.

One of the core teachings of Christ; one of the core beliefs of Christianity, is that everyone I come into contact with is my brother or sister, is my husband or wife, is my son or daughter, is my father or mother.

The Church, encompassing all peoples, all races, all ethnic groups, symbolises this. Our parish, welcoming all comers, at all times, symbolises this. At weekend masses: sitting beside persons from any background and from any country and continent, must bring this home to me. Must urge me to get to know one another, to listen to each other, to be of service to each other. The parish provides me with a wider community, a bigger Christian family, to whom I can be of service.

6th Sunday of Easter (C) 2016

We read in today's Gospel reading; 'Peace I leave with you; my peace I give to you. I do not give to you as the world gives.'

For me this peace only appeared when I slowly began accepting myself as I am - being reasonably happy with myself as I am. For years I did not realize that I was not accepting myself as I am, was not happy with myself as I am. Many factors contributed to this - family life, educational practises, local accepted attitudes, religious attitudes etc.

Although religious beliefs at that time were a contributing factor to the above attitude, it was religious beliefs (albeit more mature and reasonable religious beliefs) which initiated a change - a healing.

My gradually changing understanding of what my God was like was decisive.

To put it in a nutshell I quote from the second chapter of the Book of Genesis: 'God saw all he had made, and indeed it was very good.' So my God created me as I am. My God is happy with me as I am. Is it not churlish of me not to do the same?

And added to this, my Christianity tells me that my God respects me and even loves me as I am. Am I competent to tell my God that he is wrong?

Being content with how I am, respecting myself as I am, loving myself as I am, is the sure foundation from which I can (under the guidance of the Spirit) extend the same courtesy to my fellow human beings.

Surely to respect others I must first respect myself.
Surely to forgive others I must first forgive myself.
Surely to love others I must first love myself.

For me at least, realizing and implementing the above in my life (albeit in a very stumbling and often unsuccessful way) was the essential first step in understanding, and even tasting, the sweetness of the peace which Jesus of Nazareth offers me.

'Peace I leave with you; my peace I give to you. I do not give to you as the world gives.

The world gives peace by threat (mutual destruction), by bullying, by bombing, by suppression, by sanction, by warfare, by terrorism. Only when these things fail (as they always do eventually), or when people get weary of mutual destruction or can no longer afford the cost of suppression, does 'the world' consider talking together.

The peace of Christ is a little seed planted in my heart. If I nourish it and care for it, it will slowly grow and flourish and inspire some of those who come to know me.

The secret seems to be - get to know myself as God knows me and to respect and love myself as my God respects and loves me.

It all begins from that little seed.

How do I do this?

Anyone who seeks, sincerely and persistently, will be guided by the Holy Spirit.

Ascension (C) 2016

The Ascension of Jesus of Nazareth to God the Father, marks the end of one thing and the beginning of another thing.

It marks the end of a period when the followers of Jesus of Nazareth were instructed and guided by the actual physical presence of Jesus.

It marks the beginning of the present period when the followers of Jesus of Nazareth are cut loose from dependence on his actual and visible physical presence and guidance, and have to mature into adulthood, where they have to work out, under the guidance of the invisible Spirit, what being followers of Jesus of Nazareth means on a daily basis.

The latter is relevant, not just for the Church as a unit, but also for each individual member of the church. The Church as an organisation has much to teach me and guidance to help me, but I as an individual must also accept the responsibility of making decisions on my own with the guidance of the Spirit.

My attitude must not be 'is it allowed,' but rather is it helpful to my family, my neighbourhood, my parish, in the present circumstances.

Very often a sincere and compassionate heart can be a surer guide than rules and regulations.

Teaching emphasised by Vatican II and taken up by Pope Francis, but often overlooked by our church, is the importance of firstly informing our individual conscience and then being guided by it in our daily lives.

In the Old Testament the prophet Jeremiah foretells this and in the New Testament St. Paul emphasises its validity, and I quote from Hebrews;

"This is the covenant I will establish with the house of Israel after those days, says the Lord: I will put my laws in their minds and I will write them upon their hearts. I will be their God, and they shall be my people.

And they shall not teach, each one his fellow citizen and kinsman, saying, 'Know the Lord,' for all shall know me, from least to greatest."

Parents will be well aware, that their children, from a very early age, begin to discern right and wrong.

We are created 'in the image and likeness of God.' Consciously or unconsciously we think like God. We instinctively know right from wrong. Sin is consciously suppressing what we know to be the right thing to do or the right attitude to have, because of greed, selfishness, fear or some acquired compulsion or simple cussedness.

We are a people of the post Ascension era.

God wants me to stand on my own two feet, make my own decisions and take full responsibility for what I do and say.

Pentecost Sunday (C) 2016

St. John tells us in today's Gospel that Jesus of Nazareth wants to give us peace.

'Peace be with you.' He repeats twice before giving them the gift of the Holy Spirit.

In another place we read 'Peace I leave with you; my peace I give to you.'

And again; "I have told you this so that my joy may be in you and your joy may be complete.'

'And again; 'I speak this in the world so that they may share my joy completely.'

And St Paul; 'I rejoice and share my joy with all of you. In the same way you also should rejoice and share your joy with me.'

So Christianity is about sharing what I already possess with others.

Clearly, for Jesus of Nazareth and for St Paul, Christianity was an interior peace and joy which they already experienced and wanted to share with other people.

This peace and joy has nothing to do with good fortune or bad fortune, with possessions or lack of possessions, with sickness or health, with grief or happiness, with life or death. It is a core or kernel of peace and joy, based on a knowledge and understanding of, and trust in, one's God, which may sometimes be obscured but never extinguished.

St. Paul calls this 'the freedom of the children of God.'

If I am in any way internally self aware, I will see that in many areas I am not free. Jealousy, envy, anger, selfishness, greed, ambition, hatred etc. can dictate how I think and act. In spirituality these are called passions. To a greater or lesser extent I am a slave of these passions.

How often have I been aware that what I need to do is forgive or accommodate or compromise or give to someone in need etc, but find that I will not or cannot do so.

I am not free. I am a slave to these passions and attitudes.

Authentic Christianity will free me (albeit gradually) from this slavery and allow me the freedom to give, to forgive, to help, to console, to accommodate, to love.

This is true freedom; not what the world calls freedom.

To quote St. Paul again; 'For you were called for freedom, brothers. But do not use this freedom as an opportunity for the flesh; rather, serve one another through love.'

The ultimate freedom is to possess the freedom to love one another.

This is what Jesus of Nazareth is talking about when he tells us; 'But I say to you, love your enemies and pray for those who persecute you, so that you may be children of your Father in heaven; for he makes his sun rise on the evil and on the good, and sends rain on the righteous and on the unrighteous.'

This is true freedom - the freedom of God and of the children of God.

This was the gift given to the followers of Jesus of Nazareth on Pentecost Sunday.

It gave them the freedom to overcome their fear, their self interest, their greed and ambition for power and success and to dedicate their lives to sharing this freedom, this peace, this joy.

Is that not why we are gathered here today. To share this freedom, peace and joy with each other, not just to tell God what a fine chap he is.

Trinity Sunday (C) 2016

Today I speak on Pope Francis' letter, 'Laudato Si' which urges us to live in union, peace and co-operation with the whole of creation.

The sciences tell us that for billions of years the whole universe is on a great journey of discovery. This journey will continue for many billions of years to come and will lead we know not where.

Our Faith tells us that this journey began with the Creator and will end with the Creator.

At present, our main concern is the survival of planet Earth as a home for the great diversity of creatures it maintains.

The Creator musing to himself says;
'When he (God) established the heavens, I was there,
when he drew a circle on the face of the deep,
when he made firm the skies above,
when he established the fountains of the deep,
when he assigned to the sea its limit,
so that the waters might not transgress his command,
when he marked out the foundations of the earth,
then I was beside him, like a master worker .... and I found delight in the sons of men.'

Our Creator found delight in us human beings but does our planet Earth find delight in us any more?

Evolution is the God created engine that drives this journey of discovery which our whole planet is embarked on. This requires constant change, constant mutation, constant trial and error, constant survival of the fittest, constant extinction of some unsuccessful species.

But we have reached the stage where one species - human beings - are blindly steamrolling our way over the process of evolution, governed only by our avarice and greed.

This is true not only as regards the physical world but also the financial world, the industrial world and the political world.

This is what Pope Francis is talking about.

The way we treat the planet Earth is also symptomatic of how we treat each other. Human beings are treated as an asset, as something to be manipulated, to be exploited as simple consumers with no thought to individual and family wellbeing. The corporate world which is becoming more and more powerful, worships only at the altar of inanimate market forces and offers incense to the God called profit and dividend.

We are all affected by what is happening - pollution of rivers and oceans, global warming, climate change, the very food we eat and the air we breathe can cause sickness and death.

Pope Francis urges us to make all this our primary concern.

We all love our dividend. We all love the interest we gain on our savings; but we close our eyes to the consequences which maintaining these perks often entail. It is euphemistically called 'rationalisation' which generally entails closure of branches and brutal job losses leaving individuals and families in despair with no source of income. But profits must keep increasing and bonuses must keep rising and none of us want to accept our quota of responsibility for this. As a first step we need to change our attitude to the status quo and let this change be known.

Corpus Christi (C) 2016

There are religious orders whose principal occupation and reason for existence is adoration of the Blessed Sacrament. For instance they spend many hours daily before the Blessed Sacrament and always have some members of the community praying before the Blessed Sacrament, day and night.

This requires a special kind of person and is a special kind of vocation or calling.

Many of the clergy, when it comes to doing something special or praying for some special intention or for some particular and important outcome, immediately put on holy hours of prayer before the Blessed Sacrament or 40 hours of adoration before the Blessed Sacrament or Benediction of the Blessed Sacrament, or processions of the Blessed Sacrament around the church building or around the town.

I have to admit that I find all these activities a little bit odd.

This is a purely personal reaction and would be deprecated by most clergy.

I don't believe that Jesus of Nazareth gifted us with the Eucharist just so that we could sit or kneel before it in heartfelt contemplation.

The Eucharist is a symbol. A symbol given to me as a way of remembering (of reminding me) that my God and Creator became a human being just like me. Lived with the ups and downs of life, just like me. And died, just like I will die.

At the institution of the Eucharist at the Last Supper on Holy Thursday evening, just before Jesus of Nazareth was arrested, he gathered his followers around him for the traditional Jewish Passover Meal. During this meal together he broke from tradition. Taking a loaf of bread he blessed it, broke it into pieces, which he handed to each of his followers, and said, take this and eat it for 'this is my body which will be given up for you.' Then taking the jug of wine he poured some into each of their cups saying this is the cup of my blood which will be shed for you. Then he told them; 'do this in memory of me.'

A few important points here. Jesus spoke in the future tense; which will be given up for you, which will be shed for you. He was speaking of his coming crucifixion and death on the cross the next day - Good Friday. The separation of body and blood means death.

Do this in memory of me he instructed. In the Eucharist - the Last Supper - the Mass, they were given a way of remembering, not only his crucifixion and death, but equally important, his life among them, his actions among them, his teaching of the Kingdom of God while he lived with them.

This remembering and symbolic representing of his life, death and resurrection was to be a catalyst, propelling his followers, down the ages, to go forth, following in his footsteps, to live and proclaim his message of the Kingdom of God.

I must always remember that the Mass - the Eucharist - is not an end in itself, is not a fulfilling of an obligation, but a remembering, a celebration, propelling me out into the world to live and spread the Good News.

> The Eucharist, the Mass, does not stand alone. It is a prelude to living and action.
>
> On the other hand there is nothing odd about Eucharistic devotions that actually motivate me to action.

10TH SUNDAY OF THE YEAR (C) 2016

Jesus of Nazareth proclaimed the good news of the kingdom of God and lived it. But it was not only this that attracted huge crowds of people to him. He also performed great wonders like what we read of in today's Gospel.

The New Testament gives us two reasons for these wonders or miracles.

Firstly, compassion. In today's Gospel we read; When the Lord saw the weeping mother 'he had compassion for her and said to her, "Do not weep."'

With two blind men; Jesus stood still and called them, saying, "What do you want me to do for you?" They said to him, "Lord, let our eyes be opened." Moved with compassion, Jesus touched their eyes. Immediately they regained their sight and followed him.'

'When he went ashore, he saw a great crowd; and he had compassion for them and cured their sick.'

As you well know there are numerous other miracles or wonders (especially healing) performed by Jesus and in almost all cases the proximate motivation was compassion.

Secondly, signs: When Jesus changed the water into wine at the wedding feast at Cana we read, 'Jesus did this, the first of his signs, in Cana of Galilee, and revealed his glory; and his disciples believed in him.'

When he cured the official's son we read, 'this was the second sign that Jesus did after coming from Judea to Galilee.'

When Jesus fed the five thousand we are told; When the people saw the sign that he had done, they began to say, 'This is indeed the prophet who is to come into the world."

And after raising Lazarus from the dead we are told:

It was because they heard that he had performed this sign that the crowd went to meet him.

So we have Jesus of Nazareth responding to the everyday pain and grief that surrounded him by directly alleviating it with miracles and wondrous works.

These wondrous works were also potent signs that the Kingdom of God, which he proclaimed, had arrived. The Kingdom of God was something that couldn't tolerate pain, grief and death.

So we have a dilemma here.

We have a God who cannot tolerate pain and suffering in His Kingdom and we have a God who created the whole universe where pain, grief and death exist in abundance.

> This is the old perennial problem of trying to integrate a compassionate, merciful, loving Creator with the existence of the extreme suffering that exists in the world.
>
> Then we have Jesus of Nazareth - God himself - being tortured and brutally executed on a cross and not lifting a finger to prevent it. Not even running away and hiding.
>
> There have been many efforts at trying to explain this problem. Some of these are helpful to some people, but the problem still remains.
>
> This is an example where prayer and communion with your God is the only road to a helpful solution. I find that people who are at peace with themselves, despite much grief and suffering, are people who, in one way or another, have been granted a relationship with their Creator which seems to bring peace of mind, and acceptance of their lot.

This is a personal gift and is not transferable to, or communicable with, others. This is something I have to work at myself, and talk to God about.

Problem solved!!

11th Sunday of the Year (C) 2016

Integrating today's Gospel reading into my understanding of what my God is really like, is very important.

Simon the Pharisee was a religious leader and one would assume that many of the other guests at the meal were also in various religious roles or were at least staunchly religious.

They were taken completely by surprise by what happened and horrified by Jesus' reaction to, and treatment of, the 'sinful' woman.

Again, in Ireland last year, the religious leaders were taken by surprise and horrified by the overwhelming approval for the legalisation of same sex unions.

Our churches' questionnaire on family life, last year in England and Wales, had similar results and was roundly opposed by very many of our churches' leaders at the Synod in Rome. In today's Gospel reading Jesus of Nazareth was not indicating that her life style was morally all right. He was demonstrating God's love, welcome, acceptance and mercy for all his children irrespective of who they were or what their lifestyle was.

This is one of the things Pope Francis is trying to get across, and it is causing an equally shocked furore among religious leaders.

The attitude of Simon the Pharisee is common, within religious organisations, all over the world to this day.

There is an old adage in our church called the 'sensus fidei' or 'sensus fidelium'. It means the sense of the faith or the sense of the faithful, and refers to the general opinion of the members of our church on any issue. One time it was very important and popes would not pronounce on an important issue without first taking the pulse of the faithful on the issue. It has fallen into disuse in recent times and needs to be reinstated. A lot of current church problems would have been avoided if our leadership had listened to the 'sensus fidei.'

The latter is something Pope Francis is also trying to reactivate. Hence the questionnaire.

I and you must contemplate today's Gospel reading and try to parallel Jesus' attitude in our own attitude towards current problems and issues.

Things that immediately come to mind are immigration, the upcoming E.U. referendum, ecology, the subjection of human welfare to the profit motive, rejection and marginalisation of certain groups, etc.

Let us seek guidance in these matters as we listen to some music.

12th Sunday of the Year (C) 2016

Who do you say I am?
   Peter answered, 'the Messiah of God.'
   In Greek, 'the Messiah' is translated as 'the Christ.'
   Both words mean 'the anointed one.'
   The Messiah / the Christ was sent by God to set his people free and to initiate the Kingdom of God.
   Up to the time of Jesus of Nazareth, belief in and understanding of, the Messiah went through many phases. At the time of Jesus of Nazareth the hope of the people of Israel was that the Messiah would free them from the yoke of the Roman Empire and set up a free independent Nation, like at the time of King David.
   We read 'Jesus strictly warned them not to tell this to anyone.' This was because the Kingdom he was sent to inaugurate had nothing in common with an earthly kingdom or empire as they understood it.'
   Jesus of Nazareth was sent by God (the Father) to demonstrate by word and example what God is truly like. 'I have come down from heaven, not to do my own will, but the will of him who sent me.' And again 'be perfect as my heavenly Father is perfect' he declared.
   So the Kingdom of God which Jesus of Nazareth was sent to initiate was not a kingdom with borders or boundaries but one made up of all those who sought to live like God.
   If I want to know how my God lives I have only to look at Jesus of Nazareth and follow in his footsteps.

Jesus told them 'you know the way to the place where I am going. Thomas said to him, "Lord, we do not know where you are going. How can we know the way?" Jesus said to him, "I am the way, and the truth, and the life. No one comes to the Father except through me. If you know me, you will know my Father also. From now on you do know him and have seen him."

Philip said to him, "Lord, show us the Father, and we will be satisfied." Jesus said to him, "Have I been with you all this time, Philip, and you still do not know me? Whoever has seen me has seen the Father. How can you say, 'Show us the Father'? Do you not believe that I am in the Father and the Father is in me?"

So Christianity is following in the footsteps of Jesus of Nazareth. The Kingdom of God which Jesus inaugurated is made up of all those who decide to walk in His footsteps.

So what does this mean for me in practice, what is the nitty-gritty of following in the footsteps of Jesus of Nazareth.

> Jesus spells this out for me very clearly; 'But I say to you that listen; Love your enemies, do good to those who hate you, bless those who curse you, pray for those who abuse you.'
>
> And again, 'Do not judge, and you will not be judged; do not condemn, and you will not be condemned. Forgive, and you will be forgiven; give, and it will be given to you. A good measure, pressed down, shaken together, running over, will be put into your lap; for the measure you give will be the measure you get back.'
>
> So that's it!
>
> The Kingdom of God is the community of those people who strive to live in this way, irrespective of where they live or who they are or what organisation they belong to.
>
> Now the big question; do I belong in this company?

13th Sunday of the Year (C) 2016

Last week we looked at the type of Kingdom Jesus of Nazareth was sent to inaugurate and the type of people who belong in this Kingdom.

The standard is high. To tell us to 'be perfect as our heavenly Father is perfect' is nigh impossible. Today, on a similar vein, we are told that "No one who puts a hand to the plough and looks back is fit for the kingdom of God." The fact that you are here today indicates that you have all put your hand to the plough. Would those of you who have not looked back please raise your hand. So none of us are fit for the Kingdom of God.

Neither were any of the Apostles fit for the Kingdom of God.

Neither was Mary fit for the Kingdom of God, but, to quote herself, it was because 'the Lord has done great things for me' that made her fit for the Kingdom of God.

It was because the Lord did great things for the Apostles, for the Martyrs, for the saints, for our parents and grandparents and today for each one of us, that has or will make us, fit for the Kingdom of God.

If there was one thing that stood out in the life of Jesus of Nazareth it was his welcome for, and acceptance of, all who came to him with a humble and contrite heart. On the other hand he was repelled by the deliberately proud, self-satisfied, religious bigots of his day.

His arms were open for all those in distress or trouble. Those who felt inadequate. Those who realised that they fell short of the ideal ; those who needed help and knew it. For him the first step into the Kingdom of God was realising that of myself I can do nothing. Realising that the Kingdom was one whose members trusted totally in the compassion, mercy and help of the King. It is a kingdom of those struggling with their sins and phobias and addictions.

We have the many apparent contradictions we find in the Gospels such as; our ideas of peace and God's idea of peace, our idea of kingdom and God's idea of Kingdom, Jesus of Nazareth's insistence that we 'be perfect as your heavenly Father is perfect' as against his obvious preference for those who knew they were inadequate and sinners, etc. To digest and understand these apparent contradictions we must accept that, and I quote 'my thoughts are not your thoughts, nor are your ways my ways, says the Lord.'

I shouldn't worry too much about putting my hand to the plough and looking back as long as my other hand keeps a tight hold onto Jesus' hand.

14th Sunday of the Year (C) 2016

'After this the Lord appointed seventy others and sent them on ahead of him in pairs to every town and place where he himself intended to go.'

These seventy others weren't apostles. They were dedicated believers in Jesus of Nazareth, who had families, businesses, farms etc. to look after, and could only make brief visits to see and listen to Jesus. They were like all of you. Dedicated followers who also had other duties and responsibilities. When they were available Jesus commissioned them, using the same words as he used for the twelve apostles, to go forth and prepare the people to receive Him and his message of the Kingdom of God.

When you see a cloud rising in the west, you immediately say, 'It is going to rain'; and so it happens. And when you see the south wind blowing, you say, 'There will be scorching heat'; and it happens. You hypocrites! You know how to interpret the appearance of earth and sky, but why do you not know how to interpret the signs of the present time?

Our church is presently bemoaning the lack of vocations to the priesthood and the religious life. Money and manpower is being put into fostering such vocations. This is good and necessary. But why are we not interpreting the signs of the times? Why are we not listening to Pope Francis, who is struggling, against strong opposition, to promote the involvement of the so called laity in the life and leadership of our church?

To quote the words used in Baptism when we are anointed on the forehead with the oil of chrism. 'As Christ was anointed Priest, Prophet and King, so may you live always as a member of his body, sharing everlasting life.'

All of us have been anointed priest, prophet and king, so why are we so diffident about assuming our duties, rights and privileges?

Many of us feel nostalgia for the 'good old days' be it in the church or the state. But in reality the good old days were never like we may imagine them to have been.

The future is for those who read the signs of the times and act on them.

"To another he said, "Follow me." But he said, "Lord, first let me go and bury my father." But Jesus said to him, "Let the dead bury their own dead; but as for you, go and proclaim the kingdom of God."

I am pleased by the many of you who have responded generously to the rights and privileges gifted to you in Baptism, despite your many other commitments. But others stay withdrawn, thinking, I cannot do that or it is not necessary for me to do that. You may be surprised at the talents you possess, unknown to you, once you put your hand to the plough.

As Jesus of Nazareth, giving thanks to God his Father said; thank you, Father, Lord of heaven and earth, because you have hidden these things from the wise and the intelligent and have revealed them to infants.'

16th Sunday of the Year (C) 2016

'Mary sat beside the Lord at his feet listening to him speak. But Martha was distracted by her many tasks.'

Here we have the two sides of right spirituality.

1) The disciple sitting at the teachers feet listening attentively to his words.
2) The disciple busy in the service of others.

These two need to be combined for our Christianity to be fruitful.

This is the reason for the Sabbath. A time to ease off from my daily round of tasks and to listen to Jesus of Nazareth talking to me.

I dislike the term 'take a break.' It brings to mind a small group of people gathered round the water fountain or the coffee machine, smoking and gossiping unkindly.

If I do it correctly. If I take time to listen. This leads me to service, with greater motivation, which leads me to more listening, which in turn renews and clarifies my motivation.

Today's reading seems to assume that Mary, after listening, would move on to service with greater motivation and clarity, while Martha, whose frenetic concentration on service was getting her down, lacked the proper motivation and clarity of purpose.

So the Sabbath rest, retreats, time spent in prayer, meditation or reading the Scriptures, are not ends in themselves but one side of our Christianity. The other side is, properly motivated service to others. They are not two separate sides as such but coordinated parts of the one whole - just as my right hand and my left hand are not separate entities but integrated into the one body.

I find it very helpful to stop from time to time (five seconds, twenty seconds, one minute, five minutes) and rest in the caring and loving arms of my God, becoming conscious that we are all brothers and sisters - God's beloved children - and let my God renew and energise my motivation to continue in my service to the wellbeing of others.

If I do this often it can become a more or less permanent state of mind.

I think that this is the sort of thing Jesus of Nazareth meant when he told his followers about the necessity for them to pray always and St Paul when he spoke of praying continually, and the church, when it speaks of walking in the presence of God.

17th Sunday of the Year (C) 2016

In today's gospel reading the first part of the 'Our Father' is centred on God.

It acknowledges God as Father. Gives praise and thanks to God and prays for the growth of God's kingdom - that compassion, mercy and love become the norm in our lives.

The second part is centred on my needs.

The rest of the Gospel reading shows me how not to pray.

I must not approach God as I would a human donor; who has to have an explanation as to what I want and as to why I want it.

God, knowing me intimately and loving me dearly, already knows and fully understands all this. But God knows a few things more which I do not know or fully appreciate.

God knows whether this is good for my total wellbeing or not, and God knows whether I am ready to receive and capable of handling, what I am asking for.

We all have experienced how annoying and exasperating it is when someone keeps begging for something which we will not, or cannot, give for good and valid reasons.

I do not think that I should subject my God to this sort of treatment.

If I want to ask my God for something, then it is a good idea to ask for what I know God wants me to have - a humble, compassionate and generous heart.

Surely I will get it as soon as I am capable and willing to accept it.

Then there is also the prayer of contemplation and mysticism. I know nothing about these types of prayer and if God is calling me to this he will have to shout a good bit louder!

18TH SUNDAY OF THE YEAR (C) 2016

Today's gospel is about personal values, personal priorities.

I must ask myself, what do I want from life? What is my ambition in life?

In the religious life, an everyday examination of conscience is given much importance.

This might be just a listing of so called sins committed.

It can also be (especially as I get older) a hard look back at what makes me squirm in embarrassment and what I would wish people to know more about. This shows me clearly the things I wish I had never done or said and the things which make me happy to think about.

As I have said many times before, I do not need popes, bishops, priests or spiritual gurus to tell me what is right or wrong. I am created in the image and likeness of God, and God's way of life is imprinted in my heart.

But as St. Paul says; 'I can will what is right, but I cannot do it. For I do not do the good I want, but the evil I do not want is what I do.'

How many times have I resolved to do something my heart tells me is good and the right thing to do, but I keep putting it off. I put it on the long finger until it is forgotten or the resolve to do it is choked by other considerations.

Today's readings focus on my preoccupation with accumulating wealth. The Bible speaks of this preoccupation as a type of slavery.

Unless I regularly divest myself of some of my wealth in favour of those in need, I will find that I am literally unable to break away from this slavery in any meaningful way.

St. Paul tells us that Christ wants to set me free. Free from the yoke of slavery to sin. Free to forgive, to share, to serve, to love.

It is very clear that the financial collapse of 2008 was the result of total slavery to the accumulation of wealth at any cost. We all shared in this slavery in one way or another and we all paid the cost. But have we learned the lesson? Have we made any effort to break the bonds of this slavery?

As we read in Hebrews; 'Keep your lives free from the love of money, and be content with what you have.'

The teaching of the Bible on wealth and property is, in a nutshell; All I have is a loan given to me for a fixed time, to sustain myself and others who are in need.

And it is so convenient to forget the latter.

19th Sunday of the Year (C) 2016

Today's Gospel reading has two messages for me

Firstly; 'Do not be afraid.' Fear has no place in my relationship with my God. If I am afraid of my God then I am insulting my God in the worst way possible. If I fear that my God will punish me for not obeying him, for not serving him, for not loving him then I am treating my God as a sadistic, vengeful, person.

Think of a parent who, when a child does not obey, serve and love them as required will eject it from their home to wander homeless and penniless as a vagrant.

Is that how you think of your God?

If so then your life must be an unhappy one.

The Bible does speak of fearing God. The Bible does speak of punishment for disobeying God.

As well as telling me correctly what God's attitude to me is, the Bible also tells me what the attitude of various people was to God. Many of these people had the wrong attitude towards God. Many of them wavered from one side to another in their attitude to God. I must understand that the Bible tells me as much about what God is not like, about what people's wrong attitude to God is, as it does about the correct attitude to God. The carrot and the stick was as much in use in Biblical times as it is today, to achieve compliance. The latter is a human invention not a Divine one.

When we read in the Bible that; The fear of the Lord is the beginning of wisdom.' its meaning is the attitude of a dearly beloved child to a dearly beloved parent; The child rejects, shudders at, the very idea of doing anything which might disappoint the parent in any way. The fear of punishment does not enter in.

Secondly; With all the above in mind we understand the second message of today's Gospel reading. "Be dressed for action and have your lamps lit; be like those who are waiting for their master to return." Again here, what is visualised is a patient waiting, in joyful expectation, to greet and welcome the beloved master of the house. The master is the bearer of many gifts and good food for all.

Becoming inebriated on the job or falling asleep on the job and failing to open the door is unthinkable. Inconveniencing the beloved master in any way is unthinkable.

Again fear of punishment does not enter in.

When it comes to punishment for sin there is no need to posit a punishing God.

Being created in God's image and likeness, sin or wrongdoing is going against my very nature. It is acting in an unnatural way. This in itself brings about its own punishment.

Our jails are full to overflowing. It isn't God who put them there.

> Thousands are summoned each year to be grilled at parliamentary enquiries. It isn't God who summoned them.
>
> The courts are overflowing with people waiting for sentencing. It isn't God who hauled them to court or who will sentence them.
>
> We all know the people who are mean, who are liars, who are awkward to deal with, who are greedy, who cannot be depended on etc. and they get treated accordingly; not by God but by us.
>
> Sin, bad behaviour, comes with its own packaged punishment.

20TH SUNDAY OF THE YEAR (C) 2016

Today is the feast day of the Assumption.

This means that Mary, the mother of Jesus of Nazareth was, at the end of her lifespan here on earth, brought up body and soul into Heaven.

This was declared to be a dogma of the Catholic Church by Pope Pius X11 in 1950.

This dogma, although a very nice and suitable gesture of a son for his mother, has no particular significance, that I know of, for Christianity as a way of life.

Today is also the twentieth Sunday of the year and a continuation of the readings of the last few Sunday's, for which reason I am using these readings.

"I came to bring fire to the earth, and how I wish it were already kindled!" Fire is here used as a symbol for cleansing or purifying.

Jesus of Nazareth came to cleanse the world of hatred, envy, jealousy etc.

He calls his followers to be pure of heart; To kindle the fire of generosity, forgiveness, and love in their hearts.

There is a baptism with which I must be baptized, and how great is my anguish until it is accomplished!'

Baptism here is used to symbolise the pain and anguish of his approaching arrest and execution on a cross. He is well aware that his lifestyle and teaching, which is totally opposed to injustice and oppression of the poor and the helpless, has won him implacable enemies in the political and religious leadership. This can only result in detention and execution.

'Do you think that I have come to bring peace to the earth? No, I tell you, but rather division!'

Although His message is 'peace I leave with you; my peace I give to you' he also adds, 'I do not give to you as the world gives.'

For Jesus of Nazareth it is not peace at any cost. Peace must not compromise the word of God. Temporary peace imposed by oppression of legitimate opposition is not envisaged.

'From now on five in one household will be divided, three against two and two against three;'

If one is to 'seek first the kingdom (of God) and his righteousness' in all things, one is liable to meet opposition, even within one's own family, not to speak of in the workplace and in the wider community.

Seeking justice and fair treatment for all, is not, and never was, the recipe for universal popularity.

21st Sunday of the Year (C) 2016

Luke's Gospel presents the life of Jesus of Nazareth as a journey from Galilee to Jerusalem.

This journey is of course symbolic. Luke fits the life and teaching of Jesus of Nazareth within this literary framework of a journey from Galilee to Jerusalem.

The journey begins with His leaving home in Nazareth and the call of God at His baptism in the Jordan and ends with his arrest and execution in Jerusalem.

It is a journey of obedience to the Father's will. Not that the Father willed him to suffer and be executed on a cross, but that the Father's will was, that His life be one totally dedicated to the service and wellbeing of others. This led, inevitably, to hostility from the civic and religious powers of the time who brought about his arrest and execution to safeguard their own position and power.

So Jesus' life is depicted as a Journey. A journey of ongoing free choice - to stand by the poor and the oppressed and not to succumb to the threats and bullying of the oppressors.

We see this total commitment in the following passage, where his apostles, aware of where this commitment was leading to, tried to advise caution.

"Jesus began to show his disciples that he must go to Jerusalem and undergo great suffering and Peter took him aside and began to rebuke him, saying, God forbid it, Lord! This must never happen to you. But he turned and said to Peter, 'Get behind me, Satan!' You are a stumbling block to me; for you are setting your mind not on divine things but on human things."

The will of the Father; that is the struggle for justice and fair distribution for all, must not be modified or watered down because of fear or threats.

Today's Gospel reading is rich in examples of our efforts to modify our commitment to the will of the Father. It can be just doing enough to 'get into heaven' (whatever that means), to claiming to be Christians just because we were Baptised and appear in church the odd time.

A total commitment to the wellbeing of the poor and oppressed is not common.

Nevertheless there will be those who understand the message of Jesus of Nazareth and commit themselves to the will of the Father.

So I must not hide behind claims that I am a 'good Catholic,' that I attend Mass regularly, that I eat and drink at the Lord's Eucharistic table, that I help out in my parish etc. These are periods of R & R in the fight for justice and peace.

Lastly let me ponder the story of the good, conscientious, young man who ran up to Jesus asking, "Good teacher, what must I do to inherit eternal life?"

"Jesus, looking at him, loved him and said to him, "You are lacking in one thing. Go, sell what you have, and give to the poor and you will have treasure in heaven; then come, follow me." - Follow Him in the fight against injustice, greed, and oppression.

So we give what we can, and also fight against injustice and oppression. This is the invitation. This is the call. This is Christianity.

But who among us lives up to this call? Maybe some do. The Apostles didn't.

For I, you and the Apostles, who fail so miserably, there is the mercy of our God, the compassion of our God, the understanding of our God, the forgiveness of our God.

Nevertheless we keep striving to enter through the narrow door.

22ND SUNDAY OF THE YEAR (C) 2016

'My son, conduct your affairs with humility, and you will be loved more than a giver of gifts.'

Just think for a moment of the people you feel most comfortable with. Think of those who's company you seek out.

You will find that, by and large, they are people who can admit that they do not know everything, who accept that they can be wrong, who can apologise if the occasion demands it.

The greatest gift you can give your children is to teach them, by word and example, to accept openly that they are sometimes wrong, to apologise sincerely for their mistakes.

This is not only good advice in our everyday interaction with others at home, at work and in our social life. It is also good for our relationship with our God, and I quote;

'Humble yourself the more, the greater you are, and you will find favour with God.'

Humility is truth. Admitting I was or am wrong, apologising for mistakes, both deliberate

and accidental, is simply acknowledging openly what everyone knew to be the case anyway.

Is there anything more off-putting, more infantile, than sticking to my guns when everyone knows that I am wrong, including myself.

We Catholics, as a church, are not immune to this. For example even the most recent texts brought out this year present us with Original Sin as a theological fact when it is no longer tenable in the original, traditional, understanding of the doctrine.

Also the continued presentation of the Sacrament of Reconciliation, in its traditional understanding and practice, as the only way to forgiveness, when this is not and never was true.

'Water quenches a flaming fire, and alms atone for sins.'

Generously sharing my good fortune with those in need is another form of humility, is another form of apology. It acknowledges that what I regard as my possessions are in fact

God's possessions. It acknowledges that I have been remiss in my stewardship of God's possessions and takes steps to alleviate this fault.

Lastly, who can remain hostile towards one who gives generously?

29th Sunday of the Year (C) 2016

This Gospel reading can be quite bewildering.

We know that God fully understands our desires, needs and troubles long before we even think of asking.

We know that God is definitely not like the corrupt judge.

We know that God does not appreciate long winded and persistent prayer of petition.

"Do not babble like the pagans do, who think they will be heard because of their many words."

So what are we to make of today's gospel reading?

I think the key word is 'justice.'

In Jesus of Nazareth's day the most destitute and oppressed persons were widows.

This widow was looking for justice. She was looking for something which she had been unjustly deprived of.

She was not looking for favours, or handouts. Because she was alone with no man to support her in the patriarchal society of her day, she was helpless and had been unjustly deprived of her means of livelihood.

Seeking justice for the helpless and the oppressed was at the very heart of Jesus' ministry. This is why he was arrested and executed. Civil and religious leadership feared he would eventually threaten their privileged position and lifestyle.

I think that we can say that all of us here today are of privileged position and lifestyle.

We do not have to go to the third world to hear the plea for justice and fair dealing. It is all around us today in England.

I do not think that Jesus of Nazareth is quite content with my occasional contribution to charity and the limited volunteering of my time and expertise (good and laudable as this may be). I think He expects a more radical personal commitment and change of attitude towards my fellow human beings and towards my possessions.

A book I read recently had a little story which has stuck in my mind. I think Jesus of Nazareth would empathise with this story.

30th Sunday of the Year (C) 2016

The meaning and message of today's gospel reading is obvious and clearcut. There is no need for further clarification.

Therefore I would like to continue with the theme of last weeks homily where we saw how our present fixation on the profit motive is turning us human beings into mere pawns in the service of financial gain.

Pope Francis links this disastrous attitude towards people with an equally disastrous attitude towards the world around us. This planet on which we live and on which we are totally dependent for survival, is systematically being raped, polluted and decimated for purely economic reasons - to maintain the very high standard of living to which some of the world's human population have become accustomed. This policy is being pursued by companies and governments worldwide with disastrous consequences for the ecology of our planet. Warnings by concerned groups, by the scientific community and indeed by nature itself, are dismissed as exaggerations or as being totally wrong.

We are all beginning to see the consequences of this disregard for the planet on which we live and are totally dependent. As a young boy I could safely drink from any stream or river I came across. Today if one did that they would need to see the doctor immediately. I could breathe the air knowing it was good for me. Today the air we breathe is so polluted that it is the single biggest contributor to sickness and death. Rising sea levels threaten our coastal towns and homes.

Extreme downpours of rain are giving rise to extensive and repeated flooding. Getting rid of our waste is becoming a more and more expensive and complicated procedure. I forget how many thousand species of living things are going into extinction every year etc. etc.

Just helping the 7 billion people of the world to achieve the standard of living we enjoy is not, on its own, going to solve world poverty or destitution. People who study and understand these things tell us that for the 7 billion people of our planet to enjoy our standard of living would need 5 earth size planets to sustain it. So it is not just a case of trying to raise the world-wide standard of living to equal ours. A drastic lowering of our expectations and standard of living is also necessary to maintain such a population.

Unfortunately Pope Francis does not explicitly mention overpopulation. I think there is no doubt that overpopulation of our species is a major cause of our problem. Our planet is presently losing the struggle to sustain our present population. But this population is continuing to grow at an alarming rate. Anyone who has lived in the third world for any length of time will have witnessed the frightening population explosion of homo sapiens. There is simply just not enough space and resources to go around. Our high standard of living and extreme rate of consumption is of course a major factor.

All the above is not good news. Nevertheless we must try and take it aboard because it is true. I must try and accept the facts and think of the future of our children and grandchildren.

Pope Francis points out how difficult the task will be because the very structures and systems of governments and corporations are geared to profit making and increased consumerism.

I think the first step for me must be to really convince myself of the peril the human race is in and try to convince as many people as possible of this, especially the next generation.

If everyone understood the danger our planet is in then something might happen.

Personally I think that only God can help us to recover from our downward spiral to extinction as a species, and God's solution might be quite painful.

31st Sunday of the Year (C) 2016

Zacchaeus was an important man in the city of Jericho. He was the chief tax collector. He was the top civil servant for the Roman Empire in Jericho. He was feared because he could fix the rate of taxation for the people and businesses of Jericho. Because of this he was shown great outward respect while being secretly despised as a traitor and sinner because he worked for the hated Roman Empire. He was corrupt as all tax collectors were because he had the power to fix one's rate of taxation and could skim off the top for himself or demand favours.

He was wealthy, settled and set up for life. The future was a comfortable retirement with a nice fat nest egg.

Not the sort of person one would expect to change.

Not the sort of person one would even bother to try and change.

Imagine this wealthy, well dressed, dignified, short, fat man, waddling up the road as fast as he could ahead of the crowd, panting and slipping in his efforts to climb a small fig tree so that he could see what Jesus of Nazareth looked like!

How ridiculous can one appear!!

We can only imagine what might cause a man like Zacchaeus to do such a thing.

Perhaps, despite his position, wealth, nice lifestyle etc. he wasn't as happy as he expected to be, wasn't at peace with himself as he had hoped to be.

Whatever the reason he was prepared to expose himself to ridicule and to the vicious gossip of his many enemies so as to get a good look at Jesus of Nazareth.

We only know the result.

Zacchaeus, the rich, corrupt, selfish, tax collector has become a paradigm for change. Surely, if he could change, any one of us can change.

And everyone of us here today needs to change in one way or another, to some degree or another.

32nd Sunday of the Year (C) 2016

People who believe in life after death have always been around.

People who do not believe in life after death have always been around.

Anthropologists tell us that the very earliest human burial sites (dating some 70,000 years ago) contain artefacts in everyday usage such as weapons or household utensils etc. The obvious reason for this would be the belief that if the dead person needed these things in this life then he/she would need them in a life after death.

In the very same way belief in some sort of god or gods (the existence of invisible beings more powerful than oneself) is co-existent with the existence of human beings.

At the time of Jesus of Nazareth the group called the Sadducees believed in the existence of God but not in the resurrection of the dead.

All through the New Testament Jesus of Nazareth and his followers are most insistent not only on the existence of One God but also on the Resurrection of the dead. In fact death is treated by Christianity as being of no consequence whatever; simply as the passage from this present existence into total union with the Eternal life of God our Creator.

There is a trend in Christian theology down the centuries, and presently coming very much to the fore, that nothing which has been brought into existence by God the Creator will ever cease to exist in one form or another.

Pope Francis has embraced the sacredness of the whole of creation. "God saw all he had made and indeed it was very good." (Gen. 1; 31) He teaches us that it is necessary to respect and cherish the whole of creation as we should respect and cherish each other. Not only is this the right thing to do but also our very existence on planet Earth depends on it.

Christianity stands on the belief of the followers of Jesus of Nazareth that he had risen from the dead. Experiencing the presence of the Risen Lord turned a bunch of fearful disciples, who up to this point had really no idea of what Jesus of Nazareth was all about, into a close knit group of people willing and eager to stand up in public and declare their belief in the Risen Lord. They abandoned their previous life, travelled the known world and willingly gave their lives for the belief in Resurrection from death.

They fully realised what they were doing and the vital importance of belief in Resurrection from death. As St. Paul said "If Christ has not been raised, then empty too is our preaching; empty too, your faith."

The Church tells us that faith in Jesus of Nazareth and resurrection from death is a gift from God. Personally I find this unsatisfactory. If it is so important and so life changing why is it so haphazard? Why do so many really good people find it very difficult or impossible to believe?

I am afraid I don't have the answer.

I sometimes find it helpful to consider the alternative. I find it helpful to consider what my life would be like without a belief in God and resurrection from death. Certainly, I wouldn't be here doing the job I do. I find it better to travel in hope of reaching a pleasant, hospitable destination rather than just travelling until the car runs out of petrol.

33RD SUNDAY OF THE YEAR (C) 2016

There is a perpetual tension, in all aspects of life, between the status quo and the necessity for change. Life and growth necessarily means change. But we must decide on the pace of change and on what changes are necessary or desirable at a particular time.

At one end of the spectrum there is the total refusal to change and at the other the urge to throw everything out and start anew. The correct way is somewhere in between. But where?

Recent events in the western world indicate a dissatisfaction with the status quo and the desire for change. I think we must accept this and not only work for change, but look forward to it.

What does not change withers away and dies.

Looking back over the last sixty years of our churches' history this is bourne out. Vatican II brought a sense of freedom and the possibility of change to our church. But before this could filter down to the rank and file great effort was put into suppressing it by those who did not want any change.

We know the result - the greatest fall away from the Catholic Church in Europe since the Reformation.

Luckily we now have a leader - Pope Francis - who recognises this and is working tirelessly to reawaken the freedom and hope for change experienced during Vatican II.

The main stumbling block to the latter is clericalism, whose position and power is being threatened.

So now to what I want to say. If you want change it will have to come from you. I, and the vast majority of the clergy in the western world, are well beyond our 'sell by date.'

Pope Francis has urged national Bishops conferences to make proposals to him as to what should be done to rejuvenate the Church in their various countries. To my knowledge only one South American conference has done so and Francis has urged them to implement it. For the rest it is silence.

The mind of the laity was made very clear in the questionnaire of a few years ago. So there is no excuse.

So I reiterate, change will have to come from, and be implemented by you. Of course you are very busy. Of course you have very little time to spare. Nevertheless, real, on the ground change will have to come from you. Francis can only indicate the way.

We, the clergy are old, tired and bereft of new ideas.

So do try and come up with ideas as to what our parish should be doing and how we should be doing it.

The two big messages that Pope Francis has for us are care for the poor and oppressed and care for the whole environment of our planet Earth.

Christ the King (C) 2016

Today we approach Jesus of Nazareth as our Lord and King. John 18. 'Pilate asked him, "So you are a king?" Jesus answered, "You say that I am a king. For this I was born, and for this I came into the world, to testify to the truth. Everyone who belongs to the truth listens to my voice."

Today, economic, financial, political and social structures are as unjust, oppressive, and elitist as they ever were depending on who you are and where and how you live.

Jesus of Nazareth; Our God and Creator, is the king of truth.

Looking back over my life I can see that, by and large, I was fearful of the truth. This is partly to do with my upbringing and the mores of the time. Outward expressions of fear, love, compassion, concern, pity, pain etc. were frowned upon and, especially for men, considered to be unmanly.

The 'hard man' attitude was the image to project.

So here I am not talking about overtly telling lies but an attitude of denial that was hurtful to self and to others.

Times have changed and attitudes have changed (for example it seems to be the 'in thing to 'let it all hang out even to the point of invention) to the extent that one invents fears, love, compassion, pain etc. to appear cool.

So here I am trying to walk a thin line between both extremes. A line which, hopefully, will be authentic.

Luke 9. Then Jesus said to all, "If anyone wishes to come after me, he must deny himself and take up his cross daily and follow me."

Taking up ones cross daily and following Jesus is reiterated many times in the New Testament.

The path taken by Jesus of Nazareth was doomed to failure. This was the path of truth. The truth was that the whole world in which He lived was exploitative, oppressive, elitist and therefore unjust.

His public ministry was an outright condemnation of this not only by what he said openly but by the very way he lived with his group of followers.

Nobody in authority (religious or civil) wanted to hear or see this. It was too big a threat to their control and privilege.

This led to constant opposition and hostility from the authorities and his eventual arrest and execution.

Being the King of truth guarantees being the king of failure. Being the follower of the King of Truth guarantees failure. Try, as we should and as persistently as we can, we will never succeed in making the world fair and just. Human greed and ambition will guarantee that.

This is taking up one's cross, this is sharing the burden of Jesus' cross. This is what being a follower of Christ the King of truth means.

Being a Christian is, first and foremost, sharing in the struggle of Jesus of Nazareth to bring justice and fairness to our world. Only secondly is it about prayer, mass, sacraments, pilgrimages, adoration etc. which presuppose an already sharing in the struggle for justice.

This guarantees failure. It means that our main aim in life will fail.

It follows that as the Church of Jesus Christ we will fail in our main reason for existence. This is guaranteed. As Jesus said "My kingdom is not from this world. If my kingdom were from this world, my followers would be fighting to keep me from being handed over to the Jews. But as it is, my kingdom is not from here."

We have lost sight of this in our own lives and in the life of our church. Read any Church paper and the successes are highlighted. If I and you and our church were really following in the footsteps of Jesus of Nazareth then our stories would be a string of failures. Of the twelve Apostles, eleven were arrested and executed for opposing the accepted, oppressive, status quo. Would I not regard their lives as failures?

The Cross is a symbol of failure. What other organisation has a symbol like that! Perhaps I need to change my attitude to failure?

1st Sunday of Advent (A) 2016

We human beings, sometimes early on in life, or over the years, pick up attitudes and opinions which influence our lives to a great extent. These attitudes and opinions are generally unquestioned and unexamined and can be without foundation in reality or totally irrational.

When I started school in 1943/44 I distinctly remember the children (a minority) who were left handed getting the edge of a ruler across the knuckles for using their left hand to write. Using the left hand to write was somehow wrong although nobody knew why. Teachers were expected to teach all pupils to write of course, but only with the right hand.

It was only later, when it was realised that some people were born left handed just as others were born right handed, that this practice was stopped. Being right handed or left handed did not involve being right or wrong in any way. It was just how God created you.

After much thought and reading on the subject I am pretty sure that ones sexual orientation, be it heterosexual or homosexual, should be regarded and understood as we regard and understand left handedness or right handedness. It is the way you are. It is how God created you.

To accept this, in itself, is a big step for many people, as it is for me. This is so because of the attitudes and understanding, in society generally, as we grew up. As we know, even today in many countries and among many groups of people, homosexual orientation is a major problem.

On moral grounds religious organisations have huge problems with homosexuality. They range from outright and total condemnation to confused and fractious struggling for a solution, to self contradictory statements. The latter is well illustrated in a statement from our own Congregation for Doctrine and Faith some ten/fifteen years ago, and I quote The homosexual inclination, though not itself a sin, constitutes a tendency towards behaviour that is intrinsically evil, and therefore must be considered objectively disordered.' There was not, and still is not, an explanation as to how the homosexual inclination, though not itself a sin can be considered objectively disordered because it can be used in a sinful way. Surely one can say the same of heterosexual inclination. Do we not read every day, and hear in the news, how heterosexual inclination is used in a sinful way?

Do we not hear and see every day how all the gifts God has given us can be used in an abusive and sinful way?

Pope Francis has indicated a different attitude which our church should cultivate, when in response to questions on the matter he said "who am I to judge," much to the surprise of his questioners.

In heterosexual relations we expect that there exists a bond of love/liking, mutual respect, mutual support etc. or at least a good possibility of this. It is this which gives it meaning, makes it good for the partners and makes it Christian. Without this a heterosexual relationship is abusive, controlling, exploitative and meaningless.

Can the same standards not be applied to a homosexual relationship?

I believe that this is the way forward. This the attitude we should cultivate.

I believe that if we are to respect the works of God's hands. If we are 'to see all that God made and indeed it is very good.' If we are to respect and cherish every human being as God's beloved child. Then homophobic attitudes have no place in our thinking.

2nd Sunday of Advent (A) 2016

There is a great contrast between John the Baptist and Jesus of Nazareth.

John did all his work in one place, out in the 'desert' (uninhabited, infertile region) on the banks of the river Jordan. People came from all over Judea including from the capital city, Jerusalem, to listen to him. He did not enter the towns and villages. He preached repentance in preparation for the kingdom of God - in preparation for 'the one who is to come.' He did not move about.

In contrast Jesus of Nazareth did his work in the towns and villages of Galilee,

He was constantly on the move. His message was one of joy and celebration for he claimed that the Kingdom of God had arrived. It had been inaugurated. The kingdom of God is among you he said.

What was the big thing they had in common? They both spoke the truth. Whether it was addressed to the political and religious elite or to the poor hungry peasants of Galilee their message was the unadorned truth. As we would say they both called a spade, a spade.

Why did the political and religious leaders have them both executed? Why did the poor villagers of Nazareth try to throw Jesus off the precipice on which their village was built? Because he spoke the truth.

In short, God's forgiveness has no connection whatsoever with what I do or say or can possibly do or say.

Today we are speaking of repentance and forgiveness.

Nowhere have we been more two-faced with God than when it comes to sorrow for sin and repentance, especially in the Sacrament of Reconciliation.

Most of us grew up thinking that repentance and forgiveness was a sort of deal with God. I am sorry and then God forgives me. Like telling someone; if you say you are sorry I will forgive you.

(In recent years, The parade of important people queuing up to apologise publicly for being discovered in their wrongdoing and their assurance that 'lessons have been learned,' is the best comedy piece I have seen in a long time).

God does not forgive me because I say I am sorry. God does not forgive me because I am really and truly sorry. God does not forgive me because I am really, really, truly sorry and am determined to repair any and all damage resulting from my offences in so far as I possibly can. No.

> God forgives. Finish. Just as 'God is love' so also God is forgiveness.
>
> Remember when God appeared to Moses in the burning bush and sent him to Pharaoh to free the Israelites, Moses asked God whom he should say sent him. God replied, say '1 AM sent you'.
>
> 'I am who am'
>
> This is what I mean when I say 'God forgives.' God is forgiveness.
>
> This is how it works. It is only when I realise that I am totally forgiven and loved by My God prior to any sign or expression of sorrow or regret or repentance on my part, that I can hopefully move on to true sorrow, true regret, true repentance. On this foundation, on this realisation, on this truth only, can I begin to build a liking and even a love for my God.

This is why Jesus said, concerning the prostitute who had washed his feet with her tears and dried them with her hair :

'So I tell you, her many sins have been forgiven; hence, she has shown great love. But the one to whom little is forgiven, loves little.'

It was her realisation that her God loved and forgave her irrespective of what she had done, prior to any move on her part, that brought her to repentance and love.

The acceptance of this truth about my God, and the change of attitude it required was the most difficult thing I ever did, but how amazing the rewards.

3rd Sunday of Advent (A) 2016

Ongoing from last week's homily on repentance and forgiveness I must emphasise that God is truth, just as God is love and God is forgiveness, irrespective of what I am or say or do.

There can be no duplicity in our dealings with God. There can be no sleight of hand. Casuistry and clever arguments are mere self-delusion in the sleight of God.

God wants me to know Him/Her. That is the whole point of all revelation, be it in creation, Scripture or the Person of Jesus of Nazareth.

Knowing, in the Biblical sense, is not the same as it is understood today. Knowing in the Bible is experiencing, is loving, is to know God as one is known by God. We are told in Genesis 4 'Now the man knew his wife Eve, and she conceived and bore Cain.' This will give us some idea of the depth and fullness of meaning in the word 'know' as used in the Bible. Knowing God and loving God merge into one. This knowing is without reservation.

Knowing, and thus loving God, in this sense is well beyond my capacity.

Concerning repentance I am in the very same position. How much of my repentance is self pity? How much is self loathing? How much is fear of retribution? How much is embarrassment? How much is an insurance policy against future punishment? How much is just self assurance?

If forgiveness depended on the veracity of my repentance then I would be in a sorry state indeed.

Therefore true repentance, true reconciliation, true conversion are not within my capacity. Therefore a God of truth cannot make forgiveness depend on any repentance on my part because then there would be no forgiveness.

In the very same way God's love for me cannot be dependent on anything I can say or do because then there would be no love for me in God. How can anyone seriously say; I want you to truly love me and if you don't I will punish you! Authentic love cannot exist in these circumstances.

We cannot see, hear or touch God. Human beings cannot love, repent, or experience gratitude in a vacuum. It is the experience of being loved that awakens me to the possibility of loving. Receiving gifts opens me to the possibility of experiencing gratitude. Experiencing forgiveness awakens in me the need for repentance, contrition and reconciliation.

In 1 John we read 'We love God because he first loved us.'

God's great hope for humanity is that, experiencing His/Her infinite love, experiencing God's infinite generosity, tasting God's infinite mercy, compassion and forgiveness, we may be tempted by His/Her infinite Goodness to imitate, in some small way, this love, this generosity, this mercy, this compassion and forgiveness, in our dealings with each other.

Unfortunately, we human beings, limit our God to acting towards us as we act towards each other.

The Bible has many instances of the latter. God is often depicted by some authors or editors of the Bible as cruel, vindictive, vengeful etc. This tells us what the author's attitude and understanding of God was and not what God is actually like. People find it hard to see beyond their own attitudes, motivation, bias, and prejudice when trying to understand or describe others, especially so in the case of our God.

So today - Gaudete Sunday - let us rejoice and be glad for we are loved, forgiven and cherished by our God. All that is expected of me is some sort of acceptance and response. This is the "good news of great joy for all the people" as proclaimed by the Angels on Christmas night.

4TH SUNDAY OF ADVENT (A) 2106

Today we read in the Gospel that in the Old Testament Isaiah referred to the coming Redeerner as Immanuel which means 'God is with us.'

In the New Testament the angel instructed Joseph to name the Redeemer Jesus which means 'God saves.'

These two names tell us what the birth of Jesus of Nazareth was about.

In the Bible there is great significance given to names.

We see in the Book of Genesis how, when God had created everything he brought them to the Man (Adam) so that he could name them. This signified that they were now in the care of the man, he must look after them, care for them, they were his responsibility.

In the Baptism ceremony the first question the parents are asked is 'what name have you given your child.'

A name is something sacred. It should have significance for the namer. It is now in the care of the namer. It is now the namers responsibility.

There were ethnic groups (maybe still are) who, because of a very high infant mortality rate, did not name a child until it reached about five years old. This was a protection for the parents, family and clan. If the child reached the age of five its survival rate was much improved. Up to the point when the child was named it was not really regarded as a full person, as a member of the family or of the clan or tribe. It was a thing rather than a person. This made losing it a little less traumatic. The naming of the child changed all that. It was now a person.

This was its name. It was a member of a family, clan and tribe. Its death would now be a huge loss.

When naming a child, the name should reflect the hopes of the parents and family for this child.

It might reflect in some way what the child means to them. Maybe it should remember an ancestor whom the parents would like the child to emulate.

Picking a name from the Bible or the name of some saint whose life one admires, is, for Christians, a traditional way of professing their beliefs.

A person's name is sacred to that person.

Naming in the Bible is bound up with knowing.

Knowing in the Bible means far more than the word means to us today.

It is not just something to call one by, but tells us something of the nature of the person. When Moses asked God, at the burning bush, who he should say sent him to Pharaoh to demand that he set the Israelites free, God replied, say 'I am' sent you. This name tells us a lot about the nature of God. God lives by his own power without reference to or dependence on anything else. God is the only thing who 'is.' Everything comes from 'I am' and is dependant on 'I am.'

> So in naming our child, as Christians, we should try and keep all this in mind. The naming of the child should be part of knowing the child. Maybe it should, in some way, indicate the hopes of the family for this child. Maybe in some way it should indicate the character of this child.
>
> Please, do not come to me and say, we want to name our child 'Brexit.'

Christmas (A) 2106

"Do not be afraid; for see - I am bringing you good news of great joy for all the people."

I must admit that the 'old time religion' I was brought up on in Ireland was not good news.

After many years it gradually dawned on me that what I believed to be Christianity was not Christianity.

It eventually became clear to me that what I had been told about God was not true.

The God of love, compassion, tolerance, forgiveness which I now know was obscured by a God of judgment, intolerance, punishment and retribution.

I was presented with two totally contradictory Gods. I couldn't accept both so I rejected one and accepted the other. I have now made it my mission to bring joy and peace into our lives. To reject the false God of anger, revenge and punishment. To embrace the God of peace, joy, forgiveness, compassion, mercy and total commitment to my wellbeing. I embrace the God who loves and cherishes me as I am, who accepts me as I am, who forgives me before I even ask for forgiveness.

I am not blaming those who were instrumental in my upbringing in this way - they themselves were victims of the same disinformation.

Today we are blessed with a Pope who is trying mightily to bring joy, peace, forgiveness and freedom back into our church but he is being strongly opposed by those who use fear of God to keep control over people.

You will hear that the Bible says this and the Bible says that. If you cherry pick you can use the Bible to prove any position you wish to take. The Bible is one Book made up of many parts and written by many different people, over many centuries. But it must be read, understood and interpreted as one book. Therein lies the difficulty. Misinterpretation is common.

God is love. God is compassion. God is forgiveness. God is truth. God is justice and fair dealing.

But what has often been dished up to us is an angry God, a vengeful God, an unforgiving God, a punishing God. A God who will cast his 'beloved' children into eternal fire. If God is like that, then I want nothing to do with God.

The last thing God wants is fear. The thing which we should never experience is fear of God.

Reverence God, praise God, adore God, bless God, be filled with gratitude towards God, apologise to God but never fear God.

The good news for all the people is that we are loved by God. We are treasured by God. We are forgiven by God. We are God's beloved children and we will share in Eternal Life with our God.

So let us rejoice and be glad.

Epiphany (A) 2017

Today's Gospel reading is a theological narrative.

It is a symbolic narrative or parable with a deep theological meaning which is true for all time.

We do not ask who the Maji were or what country they came from. We do not ask how they travelled or how long they journeyed.

They were Gentiles or non Jews. They knew nothing of the Bible.

They were people who were searching. They were scientists who were seeking to understand the world around them and the cosmos. They were seeking meaning in life and creation. This is the star they were following. A star which at times was bright and beckoning and then again dim or invisible. Firstly they searched in the obvious place for a newborn king (in the royal palace of Herod) They asked questions and took advice in their search.

Eventually they discovered a little helpless child (the newborn son of a very ordinary couple). Certainly not what they were expecting. They were humble enough to bow down and worship. This outlandish behaviour can only be understood by a person who has received the gift of faith. They put their possessions at his disposal. They returned to where they came from satisfied and joyful. This foretells how, although many of the Israelites accepted Christianity, the vast majority of Christians were strangers (non Jews or Gentiles as they were called).

King Herod's reaction was quite different. He saw the possibility of a newborn king as a threat to his position and power. The chief priests and religious experts were offhand and uninterested in searching for this newborn king. He was an unwelcome nuisance. They went back to their sterile study of the scriptures and their Temple worship.

This foretells clearly the reaction of the political and religious leadership to Jesus of Nazareth.

This foretells the reaction today of the political and religious leadership to anyone who is rash enough to emulate Jesus of Nazareth (the King of the Jews) in his untiring efforts to eliminate poverty, greed and exploitation and to bring freedom and justice to our world. This foretells the reaction to anyone who criticises and continues to criticise our own indifference to the suffering, injustices, unfairness, waste, and exploitation in our own country today and tries to do something about it.

I do not like being made to feel guilty.

I do not like the boat being rocked.

2nd Sunday of the Year (A)
2017

'First of all, I hear that when you meet as a church there are divisions among you, and to a degree I believe it; When you meet in one place, then, it is not to eat the Lord's supper, for in eating, each one goes ahead with his own supper, and one goes hungry while another gets drunk. Do you not have houses in which you can eat and drink? Or do you show contempt for the church of God and make those who have nothing feel ashamed? What can I say to you? Shall I praise you? In this matter I do not praise you. For I received from the Lord what I also handed on to you, that the Lord Jesus, on the night he was handed over, took bread, and, after he had given thanks, broke it and said, "This is my body that is for you. Do this in remembrance of me." In the same way also the cup, after supper, saying, "This cup is the new covenant in my blood. Do this, as often as you drink it, in remembrance of me." For as often as you eat this bread and drink the cup, you proclaim the death of the Lord until he comes.

This is the earliest written account we have of the Last Supper.

All the Apostles and disciples of Jesus of Nazareth were practising Jews, as was Jesus himself.

The two big differences between the early Christians and Judaism was their belief in the Risen Lord and their practice of the Breaking of Bread (our Mass). In the beginning the breaking of Bread was essentially a very simple act of thanksgiving to the Creator. The Christians shared a meal of bread and wine while recounting and remembering the great things God had done, and continued to do for them. This Breaking of Bread was doing again what Jesus had done and said at the Last Supper. This doing and remembering, again and again, of the Last Supper, culminating in the arrest and execution of Jesus of Nazareth on a cross, was for them the way par excellence of remembering the lengths their God was willing to go to, in His/Her desire for peace, happiness and justice for all human beings. For the salvation of us human beings.

The reading from St. Paul shows how, even early on, abuses began to creep in to this Breaking of Bread. In some places people began bringing their own food and drink and refusing to share with the less well off, thus causing divisions and jealousy.

So to correct and prevent these and other abuses, down the centuries, the celebration of the Breaking of bread had to be regulated.

Over the centuries one thing led to another and as some of us will remember the breaking of bread became stylised, overloaded with obscure symbolism and celebrated by the priest with his back to the people in a foreign language which nobody in the congregation comprehended. For the congregation their participation consisted of their being present and 'saying their prayers.' For all any of the congregation knew the priest might have been darning his socks at the altar. Luckily for us, since Vatican II, the Breaking of Bread, has been simplified to some extent and is celebrated facing the congregation and in our native language.

Nevertheless our Breaking of Bread celebration needs further modification to make its connection with the Last Supper clearer and the English used needs a lot of work as it is too archaic and tries to say too much in too few words. Also many of the set readings are unintelligible to the normal congregation.

Anyway we have to make do with what we have until such a time as you people demand something better.

So a few pointers for adults which I find helpful.

- You come to Mass because you feel a need to thank your God for existence, for life, for health, for family, for friends and neighbours, for peace and security, for work, for the gift of faith and eternal life etc. In other words you come because you want to.
- Above all, you understand that the pinnacle of God's demonstration of His/Her love, concern and care for you is his willingness to endure death on a cross in his struggle against injustice, greed, unfettered ambition, and oppression. i.e. for your salvation.
- You understand that by his life death and resurrection he has secured for you resurrection from death and a sharing in the Eternal Life of God.
- You understand that the last supper, which Jesus celebrated with his Apostles, was the symbol of this - his total giving for your wellbeing - and was the way he wanted you to remember him.
- You understand that all this is not a private you/God exercise but the public act of thanksgiving and gratitude of God's family here in our parish congregation.
- That, in the event of there being no mass in your parish on a particular weekend, it is far more important to join with your parish in whatever service of worship they have than scooting off to a different parish, merely to fulfill an imaginary obligation.

3rd Sunday of the Year (A) 2017

Today I continue with talks on the Mass or the 'Breaking of Bread'

We were brought up to view the Mass narrowly, as an obligation to be fulfilled by each individual, with no reference to the Mass as a family outpouring of gratitude and praise to God, our Father/Mother and Creator.

One of the first things Jesus of Nazareth did when he started his public ministry was to pick 12 Apostles from among his followers.

Mark 3 "He went up the mountain and summoned those whom he wanted and they came to him. He appointed twelve (whom he also named apostles) that they might be with him."

The Apostles symbolised the gathering together of the twelve tribes of Israel - the chosen people.

These were the beginnings of the new people of God; The new family of God.

'Someone told him, "Your mother and your brothers are standing outside, asking to speak with you." But he said in reply to the one who told him, "Who is my mother? Who are my brothers?" And stretching out his hand toward his disciples, he said, "Here are my mother and my brothers. For whoever does the will of my heavenly Father is my brother, and sister, and mother."

I now quote from Jn. & Matt regarding the first Mass-the Last Supper.

'He said to them, "I have eagerly desired to eat this Passover with you before I suffer."'

'So the disciples did as Jesus had directed them, and they prepared the Passover meal. When it was evening, he took his place with the twelve.'

The Passover meal was a family affair but Jesus celebrated the Passover feast (the Last Supper) not with his mother and relatives but with his new family (the twelve Apostles).

We Christians here are our new family. We too (like Jesus of Nazareth) celebrate the passover feast, the Last Supper, the Mass, with our new family - those who do the will of our heavenly Father.

When the Last Supper, the Mass, was over Jesus went to the Garden of Gethsemane where he prayed alone, privately, to the Father. He did not do this at the Last supper. The Last Supper was a family celebration.

This is very important.

The heart of Christianity, the basis of the universal church, is the local parish community of believers. This is God's family in this particular place. This is my and your family in this particular place. Our church authorities have been striving for years to set up Deanery and diocesan pastoral councils. It has never worked and will never work. They do not represent a cohesive community. They are not a worshipping community. They have no sense of family.

On the other hand the parish pastoral councils work well. They have cohesion and represent a worshipping community or family.

This is the very basis of our Church.

I abhor the closing of parish places of worship just because there is no resident priest or no regular weekend mass.

You can have a vibrant, cohesive, worshipping community without a resident priest or a regular weekend Mass. This has been proved to be so in countless countries all over the world. You may not have as many members as when there is a resident priest and a regular weekend mass but you will have a strong nucleus of believing, worshipping Christians which can easily expand when conditions change.

There is no reason why a lay person should not conduct a weekend service for the parish community if no priest were available, rather that breaking up the parish family to seek Mass elsewhere. It is the worshipping parish family, be it with or without Mass, which pleases God our Father.

Do not abandon your parish family celebration just because you want to get in mass - to fulfill an imaginary obligation.

4TH SUNDAY OF THE YEAR (A) 2017

We continue with our talks on the 'Breaking of Bread'. Just imagine a Family celebration, be it to welcome a newborn member, to bid a final farewell to an aged member who has passed on, to celebrate a new marriage or a jubilee or a Christmas get together. Imagine the sort of atmosphere there would be if there were tensions between members of the family, unresolved disputes, even overt bickering and dislikes. What would your reaction be? 'Never again will I attend such a farcical event,' you would resolve. And you would be right. We always begin our celebration of the 'Breaking of Bread' with a rite of reconciliation. Our celebration of the Breaking of Bread is a travesty, a farcical exercise, should there exist tensions, disputes, active dislikes, bickering, bitterness, among us. Even should other members of God's celebrating family know nothing of this situation it effects us all because Our God, who's love, generosity, compassion and forgiveness we are celebrating, knows all about it, and is hugely affected by it. Just imagine you are enjoying your favourite salad and then you come across a fat snail happily munching away!! I must not deceive myself that the Breaking of Bread is of the slightest benefit to me or to my God if I am actively nourishing dislike or hatred towards anyone or any group of people, be they members of the congregation or not. I am just the slug in the salad. So I cannot over-emphasise the importance of reconciliation and mutual forgiveness as we gather for the

Breaking of Bread. Reconciliation and mutual forgiveness brings peace and joy to our lives. It lifts the dark veil and burden of dislike, jealousy, and desiring revenge, from our shoulders. Should I humbly and seriously recognise and acknowledge my faults and failings and truly desire reconciliation and offer forgiveness, then I will receive these gifts from my God as soon as I am capable of accepting them. Then I am free to lift up my voice, in company with the rest of God's family, in praise and thanksgiving to our God, as we say or sing together, 'Glory to God in the highest and on earth peace to people of good will.' Then we sit and listen to the word of God in the readings and the homily.

5th Sunday of the Year (A) 2017

Today we continue with our talks on the Mass. The purpose of the readings and the homily is to strengthen our sense of gratitude and our desire to express our thanks and praise to our God; which was our reason for attending Mass in the first place. In theory the readings from the Bible illustrate the theme of this particular Mass which is expressed in the collect or opening prayer which immediately precedes the readings. This link between today's opening prayer and the readings is fairly evident. Often it is not. The link is always there but too often it is only evident to the student of Liturgy and the Scripture scholar. This link and theme is supposed to be brought forth and explained in the homily but very often it would require about a half hour or more to do this adequately. It also presumes a lot of Biblical and liturgical knowledge which one rarely encounters. Since this link is so often obscure, we, the celebrating family of God, will often have to strengthen our sense of gratitude to our God by recalling privately the good things God has done for me - bringing me into existence, calling me out of darkness into his own wonderful light, giving me the free gift of faith, granting me resurrection from death and a sharing in God's own eternal life. Then, to formalise this recalling of God's many gifts, we recite, all together, the profession of our faith - the Creed. Here ends the first part of the Mass - the preparation for Mass. So what I have said so far is to explain the thinking behind the first part of the mass and how I and you should try to make it our own, so that we can proceed to the second part of the Mass with the right disposition and outlook - which is an overwhelming desire to give thanks to God, our Father, Creator and Saviour.

6th Sunday of the Year (A) 2017

We continue with the talks on the Mass.

Having completed the first part of the Mass, we are anxious to forge ahead and demonstrate to our God how grateful we are for what our God has done for us.

The greatest way to thank someone for gifts received is to reciprocate with something which the giver of the gift has not got and very much desires.

We were brought up to believe that God has everything. But that is not true.

God is our Father and our Mother. What does a parent desire most in life? Above all else a parent desires the gratitude, respect, appreciation and if possible, the love of their children.

This is something which the parent has not yet got or has not yet received the fullness of. It is something which the parent cannot get a surfeit of. It is something which makes up for, which makes worth while, all the sacrifices, heartache and worry of child rearing. It brings fulfillment and joy to the parent.

God is my parent. My God can never get a surfeit of my gratitude, respect and love. It is the only thing my God desires from me and has not yet got or has not yet got a fullness of.

Now we move on to the second part of the mass - the bringing of the gifts.

What are these gifts? What is actually and visibly brought to the altar is bread and wine.

These are symbols. Bread and wine are food and drink. Food and drink are the two absolute necessities for life and wellbeing. By offering our God these things I am saying to God 'I offer you my very life and being as a symbol of my gratitude for what you have done for me. From now on my life will be lived through, with and in Christ, in gratitude for your gifts to me - existence, life, resurrection from death and sharing in your eternal life,' etc.

The offertory procession is a time of decision. Deciding for Christ. Breaking from a way of life that separates me from Christ. Deciding to try and abandon my hostilities, my envies, my jealousies, my greed, my selfishness and self - absorption. Deciding to try to be forgiving, to be tolerant, generous and kind.

Mentally, I place these decisions for Christ in the hands of the bearers of the bread and wine, to be placed on the altar with the bread and wine, as an expression of my gratitude to my God. This, of course, is done in symbols. Symbols which I understand and which are meaningful to me.

In short, what I am doing and saying during the offertory is placing myself on the altar, with the bread and wine, as an offering to my God, for God to do with as God wishes. This is the sign or symbol of my gratitude. This is my way of saying thank you to my God and my Creator.

So the offertory procession is not for looking at the people who bring the gifts or seeing what they are wearing. The offertory procession is the time when I offer to my God something of myself as a sign of my gratitude.

The presider - the president - the priest, then takes the bread and wine, and raising them up offers them to our God as gifts brought by His family, here present, in gratitude for God's goodness.

Then the priest says Pray, brethren, that our sacrifice may be acceptable to God, the almighty Father.' And all of you, God's family here present, respond with one voice; 'May the

Lord accept the sacrifice at your hands for the praise and glory of his name, for our good, and the good of all his holy church.'

Our sacrifice, our gifts, are always acceptable to our God as long as they are sincere and authentic and not just empty promises.

7th Sunday of the Year (A) 2017

We now come to the central part of the Mass.

This is when we offer praise and thanks to God our Father and Creator, through, in union with and in, Jesus Christ. We start with the preface, which like any preface is an introduction to what is to come.

The Lord be with you

Lift up your hearts

Let us give thanks to the Lord our God

After the preface we start the Canon of the Mass.

This is when we enter the realm of mystery. Thousands of books have been written, down the ages, about how this works but the element of mystery still remains.

It is all to do with Holy Thursday evening (the Last Supper) through to Easter Sunday morning (the Resurrection).

These three days encapsulated the reason for, the meaning of, and the results of, the Incarnation.

For the two or three years of his public ministry, how Jesus of Nazareth lived, what he said and did throughout Galilee, guaranteed him the enmity of the political and religious leadership of the land. If today, I and you were to live, act and speak as He did, we too would incur the enmity of the political and religious leadership of this land.

He knew this. His Apostles and followers knew this. His mother and relations knew this.

His mother tried to talk sense to him. His relatives tried to talk sense to him. His apostles tried to talk sense to him and prevent him from going to Jerusalem. He could have quietly slipped away into any one of the neighbouring countries and lain low for a couple of years or so until the authorities forgot about him.

But that would mean surrendering to the forces of injustice, to the forces of oppression. Then the forces of evil would have vanquished him. The forces of evil would have won over the forces of good. Hatred would have defeated love, intolerance would have overcome tolerance, vengeance would have suppressed forgiveness.

So He remained true to the will of His Father irrespective of the consequences for Himself.

He lived as God lives, right up to the end.

And just as the forces of evil, injustice and oppression were congratulating themselves for their success in conquering Him and what He stood for, He arose triumphant from the tomb to lead his Apostles and followers and us today into His Kingdom of light, love and mutual forgiveness and to share in the eternal life of the Father.

This is what the canon of the Mass is about. It makes present for us today the events of Holy Thursday evening to Easter Sunday morning. We are able to relive these events in symbol. We are able to participate in and witness these events in signs.

This is a mystery.

We do it because He, Jesus of Nazareth, told us to do what He did at the Last Supper in memory of Him. In memory of his whole life among us. And especially in memory of his last three days.

At the Last Supper he did, in a symbolic way, what was about to happen to him in reality, starting that evening in the Garden of Gethsemane.

8th Sunday of the Year (A) 2017

Last week we spoke about the Canon of the Mass.

The Canon of the Mass makes present again, for our benefit today, the events of the Last Supper on Holy Thursday evening. The bread and wine - things essential for our life and wellbeing and symbolising the offering of our lives and possessions to our God - are changed into the Body and Blood of Jesus Christ. The separation of body and blood signifies the execution which Jesus underwent on Good Friday on a cross.

During the Canon, as well as following the words spoken by the priest, we might find it helpful to picture ourselves reclining at table with Jesus and the Apostles and participating in what is happening. The Apostles, although well aware of the danger they were in from the authorities while they were in Jerusalem, were unaware of events about to happen and the significance of what they were taking part in. We, on the other hand, are well aware of what is happening and of what is about to happen and their significance. The changing of the bread and wine into the body and blood of Christ signified his death on the cross which in turn signified the lengths our God was willing to go to in pursuit of our total wellbeing and in his stand in the fight against injustice and oppression. This he has asked me to do in remembrance of His trust-wordiness, faithfulness and total dedication to my welfare.

During the elevation of the body and blood of Christ after the words of consecration (the elevation of the bread and wine) it can be helpful to look on the crucifix and ask myself if this man, Jesus of Nazareth, who is willing to go to such extremes in pursuit of my total welfare, can be trusted. What more could he realistically do to win my total confidence in him and in his promises?

Should I not ask myself if the above is not sufficient to awaken in me a deep and abiding sense of gratitude to my God.

(As an aside, at this stage, it might also be helpful to consider how such a God could possibly be confused with the judgmental, accusatory and punishing god many of us were brought up to believe in).

The concluding part of the canon is when our offerings of thanksgiving now incorporated, or changed, into the total self offering of Jesus of Nazareth on the cross is raised up by the priest and presented to God our Father as the ultimate expression of our gratitude.

Raising up the Body and Blood of Jesus of Nazareth and our self - offering the priest intones:

'Through him, and with him, and in him, 0 God, almighty father, in the unity of the Holy Spirit, all glory and honour is yours, for ever and ever.' And God's whole family here present respond all together in a joyous chorus; 'Amen.' This is called the great Amen and signifies our total agreement with, participation in and response to, all we have done and said. We then move on directly to the Communion.

The Communion is God's response to our gifts of gratitude to Him/Her.

God receives our gifts (signified by bread and wine). In doing so they are incorporated with, changed into, the self giving (the gifts) of Jesus of Nazareth and offered to us (God's family here present) as our food and drink. This food and drink is now God's only begotten son. This unites us with God the Son and thus unites us with the Holy Trinity. It makes us full participants in the life of God. It makes us participants in the eternal life of God.

This means that symbolically, spiritually, we have already entered into the Eternal Life of God.

We are already in Heaven but cannot experience it physically until our bodies are glorified at the resurrection of the dead.

Receiving Holy Communion is a time of realisation. Realising that we are already one with our God, have already entered into Eternal Life together with and in unity with all our brothers and sisters here present and throughout the world and from all times, past, present and future.

Realising that we should now treat each other as fellow saints in heaven and as God's beloved children. Realising that the promises of our God are already fulfilled in our lives in spiritual reality.

For the last seven weeks I have talked on the Mass. There is a lot more to be said about the Mass and many more, and different, approaches. I have given you, in these seven homilies, what I myself have found helpful. Some of it is not easily understood so I recommend that if you are serious about learning more about the Mass and about how you might participate more fully in the Mass I would recommend a rereading of these homilies.

1st Sunday of Lent (A) 2017

Today's gospel reading illustrates symbolically the temptations that Jesus of Nazareth had to contend with all his life.

On examination we will find that they are the very same temptations every one of us has to deal with also, in one way or another, throughout our lives.

The first is the temptation to put my physical desires before the wellbeing of others. To put my self interest first. It concerns my physical appetites. Comfort, eating and drinking, sexual desire, dress, how I look, possessions. As usual, all these appetites are in themselves good and God given gifts. The problem is my allowing all or some of them to rule my life. I allow myself to become the slave of one or some of these appetites. Even worse, it damages or even ruins the lives of those closest to me. Galatians 5. "I say, then: live by the Spirit and you will certainly not gratify the desire of the flesh.... Now the works of the flesh are obvious: immorality, impurity, licentiousness, idolatry, sorcery, hatreds, rivalry, jealousy, outbursts of fury, acts of selfishness, dissensions, factions.... In contrast, the fruit of the Spirit is love, joy, peace, patience, kindness, generosity, faithfulness, gentleness, self-control."

The second temptation is particularly applicable to religious leadership. Using God or the Church to promote ones own importance is a constant temptation. Religious organisations are tempted to put their own glorification, their own interests, before the glory of God. Church leaders can try and exercise control over everyday matters over which they have been given no authority. For example.......Church authorities have been given authority to lead people to God. They have been given authority to selflessly seek the total wellbeing of the ordinary members. The temptation is to overstep this. This can be true of all human organisations of course. The party, the company, the club, the religious organisation, can become more important than the members it is supposed to serve. People in leadership roles insist on clinging to power when well past their sell by date. I don't think our Church or our parish should seek to publicise the good work that we do. I don't think that, alluring as it can be, we should be speaking of how good we think we are, how well we think we are doing, what we think we have accomplished. A good antidote to this acclaim seeking is to read Mark 10: 17-22. "As he was setting out on a journey, a man ran up, knelt down before him, and asked him, "Good teacher, what must I do to inherit eternal life?" Jesus answered him, ... You know the commandments: 'You shall not kill; you shall not commit adultery; you shall not steal; you shall not bear false witness; you shall not defraud; honour your father and your mother. He replied and said to him, "Teacher, all of these I have observed from my youth. Jesus, looking at him, loved him and said to him, "You are lacking in one thing. Go, sell what you have, and give to the poor and you will have treasure in heaven; then come, follow me. At that statement his face fell, and he went away sad, for he had many possessions."

The third temptation is the allure of power, of control, be it in the home, the church, the country or the world. Just look at our world today or any day. Is not the desire for more power, for more control, behind every military, diplomatic, political and economic move. Within our own church there is a struggle for control. Losing control is a great fear in each and every one of us.

> Mark 9. 'Then Jesus sat down, called the Twelve, and said to them, "If anyone wishes to be first, he shall be the last of all and the servant of all."

Luke 6. "You call me 'teacher' and 'master,' and rightly so, for indeed I am. If I, therefore, the master and teacher, have washed your feet, you ought to wash one another's feet. I have given you a model to follow, so that as I have done for you, you should also do."

I don't think that, during this Lenten season, I will run out of issues that need to be addressed in my life.

2nd Sunday of Lent (A) 2017

Today's Gospel reading is full of symbolism. Without understanding the meaning of these symbols it doesn't make much sense. Jesus goes up a high mountain. Jesus is often depicted as going, up a mountain or hill when he wishes to make an important speech or perform an important action. The mountain signifies a place of revelation. It brings to mind mount Sinai where God appeared to Moses and to the people of Israel. Where he made a covenant with them and gave them the ten commandments. Where his presence was signified by peals of thunder, flashes of lightning and dense clouds. It does not necessarily mean that he actually climbed all these mountains or hills. If it did, then he was quite a mountaineer. He brought along Peter, James and John to witness what was to happen. He was transfigured in their sight; his face and clothes shining brightly. Moses and Elijah appeared with him, talking with him. Moses represents the laws of the Old Testament and Elijah the prophesy of the Old Testament. Moses and Elijah were not transfigured. This signifies that Jesus was more important than Moses and Elijah. In the Old Testament nobody was more important than Moses and Elijah except God. Peter, missing this significance, suggested that they build three shelters one for Moses, one for Elijah and one for Jesus. (This assumes that Peter regarded them as equals.) This building of shelters refers to the very important Jewish feast of Tabernacles which happened at harvest time every year when the grape and olive pickers lived in little shelters in the fields until the harvest was gathered. It was a time of joy and camaraderie. It harkened back to when the Israelites wandered in the desert for forty years and lived in temporary shelters. Peter had no sooner finished speaking when a bright cloud enveloped them (the cloud signifying the presence of God) and a voice from the cloud said "this is my son, listen to him." this also correcting Peter's assumption that Jesus, Moses and Elijah were equals). The great teachers of the Old Testament were Moses and Elijah. Now God has replaced them by sending His own Son to be our teacher and exemplar. The one who must be listened to is now Jesus of Nazareth and not Moses or Elijah. The three Apostles were terrified and fell face down to the ground. But Jesus came and touched them telling them not to be afraid. Jesus touched the sick and brought them healing and joy. Here his touch frees his Apostles from fear of the God, often depicted in the Old Testament as vengeful, cruel and judgmental. The God of Jesus was 'Abba' the beloved parent. This clash between the God of Moses (the God of Law) and the God of Jesus of Nazareth (the God of Mercy) was a major problem in the early church. The first council of the Church (the council of Jerusalem) was devoted to solving this clash of opinion and attitude. One section of the church (Jewish and conservative) wanted Christians to observe all the traditional laws and regulations of the Old Testament (putting new wine into old wineskins, as Jesus himself described it). The other section (mostly Gentiles or non Jews) wanted none of this, as they regarded such traditions and regulations as irrelevant. It is uncanny that we have the very same problem in our church today. Pope Francis and his followers want us to put the new wine (Christianity) into new wineskins. A group of cardinals, bishops, priests and some lay people want to hold on to the old wineskins at any cost. That is basically what the present debate and contention in our church is all about. This debate and contention is not necessarily bad. In fact it is good and healthy - as long as my side wins!!!

3rd Sunday of Lent (A) 2017

Today's Gospel reading is so packed with symbolism, with references to the tribal history of Israel, with allusions to traditional practices, gender inequality, and historical tribal animosities that I will not even try to make sense of it for you. That is unless you have a couple of hours to spare. A great theme or symbol in the Bible is water. For areas like the middle east which are desert, semi-arid or subject to periodic and prolonged droughts, water is very much bound up with life and health. People are accustomed to travelling long distances to obtain water. It is a great blessing, equivalent to life itself. Having a constant and dependable source of water was a very great gift indeed. Even here in England if you have ever experienced dry taps for a short period you will get some idea of the importance of water in our lives. We have all experienced the rejuvenating effects of an early morning shower. Jesus uses this constant preoccupation with water in his teaching and parables. "Jesus answered and said to her, "Everyone who drinks this water will be thirsty again; but whoever drinks the water I shall give will never thirst; the water I shall give will become in him a spring of water welling up to eternal life."The woman said to him, "Sir, give me this water, so that I may not be thirsty or have to keep coming here to draw water." We all have a great thirst for love, for compassion, for recognition, for appreciation, for respect. We cannot get enough of these things. The lack or denial of these things, especially as we grow up, can have grave consequences in our lives. Can cause great damage. Jesus of Nazareth claims to have, and freely offers us, all these things. As he said "whoever drinks the water I shall give will never thirst." But do I have the bucket to lower into the well of living water? There always seems to be this hitch. God's gifts are there before me. They are freely offered. But I lack the motivation, the ability, the will, the courage, to reach out and take them. I do not have the bucket and am not willing to go to the trouble of going and getting one. I instinctively understand that accepting God's living water will mean surrendering my life to God.

Handing over control to God. Saying goodbye to self-interest. As Jesus said "My food is to do the will of the one who sent me." But I don't want this. I am not ready for this. I like to dip in and out as I feel like it. So what's the solution? I don't know. I am in the same boat as the rest of you. The saints and Jesus of Nazareth tell us that handing over control to God is the path to true freedom - freedom to love and to be loved.

4th Sunday of Lent (A) 2017

Today's Gospel reading is a fascinating and detailed account of the Pharisaic mindset. One's very erudition in a subject can blind one to reason and right judgment. One's expertise is one's pride. These two combined to bring tunnel vision and refusal to see the obvious. Today's Gospel is about seeing. A blind man, born to darkness all his life, sees. The Pharisees, as a group, priding themselves on their knowledge of the Sacred Scriptures and their expertise in distinguishing right from wrong and truth from falsehood are blind to the obvious. If I think carefully and truthfully over my life I can find occasions when I too have fallen into the same trap. I know what to do, I understand the situation, I know who is at fault, only I can solve the problem, my line of reasoning is the correct one, my response was the only possible response, I know right from wrong etc. (Every taxi driver in the country knows the solution to all the country's problems) Looking back now I can feel the prods of guilt, the uncomfortable waves of embarrassment, at my failure or deliberate refusal, to see. Parallels of today's Gospel can be seen all around us in disputes between individuals, companies, tribes, nations, political parties, churches etc. not only between them but internally also. We Catholics must not, as a church or as individuals, be too strident in our claims to being The One True Church.' History shows, as does our own experience, that our claimed oneness and truthfulness is a well patched garment. Today's Gospel reading illustrates nicely the words of Jesus of Nazareth; "I give praise to you, Father, Lord of heaven and earth, for although you have hidden these things from the wise and the learned you have revealed them to the childlike." It is well known that one can find more faith in the pew at the back of the church than in the book lined study of the theologian, the parish priest, the archbishop or the cardinal. The religious Pharisees answered (the once blind man) and said to him, "You were born totally in sin, and are you trying to teach us?" Then they threw him out." 'Threw him out' was not just telling him to 'get the hell out of here', it was a formal excommunication from Judaism. Jesus hearing this went looking for him until he found him. Having spoken together the man said; "Lord I believe", and he worshipped him. Jesus did not even bother to see the Pharisees. They were blind and couldn't see.

5th Sunday of Lent (A) 2017

Today I talk about our spiritual life. For hundreds of years our Christianity has based its spirituality on the monastic model of spirituality. A bunch of men or women living together in community (in a convent or monastery), spending maybe four, five, six hours each day in prayer and meditation, was seen as the ideal way of life for a Christian. It was regarded as the best and most spiritual way to live. This left 95%-99% of christians struggling with a way of life which was regarded as basically inimical to spiritual development, that is to having a close relationship with God. One was encouraged, even required, to set time aside for prayer, meditation, the mass, sacraments and other cultic practises in order to re-energise ones spiritual life. Just like recharging a battery. Few, immersed in the struggles, joys, duties and responsibilities of family life had the opportunity or the desire to do this on any regular basis. In this way everyday daily life became detached from the spiritual life. Became detached from the things of God. My first consciousness of an alternative, and for me, more attractive, spiritual life, came when, in the nineteen fifties I read a book by an American parish priest. Lacking the time or energy for the approved monastic style of spirituality he talked of making his everyday parish activities his prayer and his spiritual nourishment. For example in those days before Eucharistic Ministers were thought of he had to do a lot of bringing communion to the elderly and the housebound. So instead of becoming hassled and annoyed with driving in city traffic and rushing to make time for the required periods of prayer, he would belt out the hymn 'Sweet Sacrament Divine' at the top of his voice as he drove along. This not only calmed him down physically but also gave him more spiritual nourishment than the required periods of prayer which he constantly failed to perform. In other words he made his work as parish priest, with and among his parishioners, his prayer and source of spiritual nourishment. I too will always be trying to play catch-up, always be experiencing a spiritual lacuna in my life, always feeling that I should be doing something else, someplace else, until such a time as I make my everyday life to be my prayer life and my spiritual life also. For example delivering your children to school in the morning and collecting them in the afternoon can be a hassle, or on the other hand, it can be doing exactly what you should be doing at this particular time, what God wants you to be doing at this particular time, what is the very most important thing for you to be doing at this time. Doing it with good humour, a grateful heart, and gentle demeanour is your prayer at this particular time. That is where you get your spiritual nourishment at this time. Extending this attitude to everything I do and say every day is, I think, the way for us. What I should be doing or have to be doing at this particular time in this particular place must be my prayer and my source of spiritual nourishment. I do it in union with my God by dipping in and out of the presence of my God, even if just momentarily, from time to time. This attitude of mind is also known as walking in the presence of God - living in the presence of God. To set aside time for formal prayer is good and highly recommended but not always achievable, even in one's own home. Making my everyday activities my prayer, turns my whole day into a prayer and keeps the presence of my God at least in the background of my mind and consciousness. With some effort I may find myself living my whole day in the presence of my God, even when the amount of time when I am consciously in communication with God may be relatively short. This type of spirituality can work for me whether I am lecturing in philosophy or shovelling manure.

Holy Thursday (A) 2017

Today is Holy Thursday. Today is the start of the Last Supper, arrest, trial, sentencing, execution, burial and resurrection of Jesus of Nazareth – God made Man. Today's ceremony is a representation of His Last Supper. His Last Supper is a symbolic enactment of the events of Thursday evening through to Sunday morning. It is a re-enactment in signs and symbols of the latter events. It is the way he gave us to remember Him and these events. 'Do this in memory of me' he said. Today I want to highlight one aspect of receiving Holy Communion which is generally not emphasised. The consecration of the bread and wine separately symbolises the death of Jesus. Separation of body and blood inevitably brings death. Just before Communion the priest drops a small piece of the host into the chalice while saying 'May this mingling of the body and blood of our Lord Jesus Christ bring eternal life to us who receive it.' This symbolises the resurrection - the reunion of body and blood symbolises the return of life. So when I receive Communion I am united with the Risen Lord - with the Lord who is now seated at the right hand of the Father in Eternal Life. In more mundane terms it is being given the title deed to the house; to the property. It is now mine. I am already living in Eternal life. I am already a sharer in the Eternal Life of the Father just as Christ is a sharer in the Eternal Life of the Father. Receiving the Eucharist symbolises an already existing situation. Holy Communion symbolises my already possession of eternal life. The actual giving of eternal life now, and the guarantee of the future possession of eternal life. This sounds funny but when I receive Communion I sometimes (in my own mind) wander around in Eternal Life greeting my deceased relatives and friends and chatting with them. 'Surfing the cloud' as you might say. (Or maybe I am just a candidate for the psychiatric ward!!) So receiving The Eucharist, plants me spiritually and solidly in Eternal Life - in union with my God - I await my physical resurrection to experience this with my physical senses. Christianity is living out this spiritual reality in my daily life. Struggling to get across to the Apostles what Christianity means in practice, Jesus jumped up, grabbed a basin of water and a towel and washed their feet. 'I have given you an example he said.' It is a pipe dream or it is what gives meaning and purpose to life.

Easter Sunday (A) 2017

Easter is above all, a festival of light. This light signifies the clarity and understanding brought to us by the teaching and example of Jesus Christ., At the time of Jesus it was important to determine the arrival of daybreak when the first offerings were to be made in the temple. A rabbi asked his students what criteria might be used to determine that the night had ended. One student said the night had ended when there was enough light to tell a goat from a sheep. Another said when you could distinguish an apple tree from a fig tree. The rabbi gave this answer: 'A new day has arrived when you can look at a human face, and see a brother or a sister. If you are unable to see a brother or a sister in every human face, you are still in the darkness of night.' How do my present day attitudes look in this light? Has a new day arrived for me?

2nd Sunday of Easter (A) 2017

'Jesus said to him. Have you believed because you have seen me? Blessed are those who have not seen and yet have come to believe.' It is not just Thomas who found it hard to believe that Jesus of Nazareth had risen from the dead. All the Apostles had the same problem. We read; 'When he had risen, early on the first day of the week, he appeared first to Mary Magdalene. She went and told his companions who were mourning and weeping. When they heard that he was alive and had been seen by her, they did not believe.' The eleven disciples went to Galilee, to the mountain to which Jesus had ordered them. When they saw him, they worshiped, but they doubted.' Then they returned from the tomb and announced all these things to the eleven and to all the others. The women were Mary Magdalene, Joanna, and Mary the mother of James; the others who accompanied them also told this to the apostles, but their story seemed like nonsense and they did not believe them.' The Apostles had to see or at least experience the presence of the Risen Lord in some way before they could believe. It was not sufficient for them to be told. I suppose there are people who can believe in the Risen Lord just because they have been told by people they can trust. There are people who can believe in the Risen Lord (in God) by their power of deduction, reasoning and logic. Many act as if they believe because it is the safest option.

But for most of us our belief is, at least, halfhearted unless we have had some experience of the Risen Lord. These experiences can be as different as the persons who experience them and can be meaningless if explained to others. They are personal to the person. It is very often through suffering, rejection, failure and other types of distress that we receive these experiences. It can be an ability to forgive, the diminution of anger or hurt, the ability to love or the realisation of being loved etc. etc. I do not know if one should actively seek or pray for such an experience. It seems that our God visits these experiences on his beloved children in his own good time and when they are capable of receiving them. The general idea is to keep the door open at all times.

3rd Sunday of Easter (A) 2017

For many years I was plagued by the ogre of obligation. Religion for me was a plethora of obligations to be fulfilled. This attitude and belief was nurtured by those plagued by the same ogre. I now believe that this is the devils greatest tool for denigrating God and destroying the peace and joy which worshiping God should bring. It presents God as a demanding taskmaster who punishes for noncompliance. Nothing is further from the truth.

Another way of looking at it is that an obligation is only an obligation if I do not want to do it.

The root of the problem seems to be anthropomorphism. That is attributing to God our own human attitudes and mores, as for instance, equating God with our own kings, emperors, rulers etc.

Within our church (and all churches and religions, as in politics and all social organisations) we have the people who believe that members must be compelled and required to do the right thing in all aspects of life by passing laws which must be obeyed under pain of punishment. This is what I mean by the ogre of obligation. It deprives a person of freedom by instilling the fear of punishment for non compliance. One can see the point of this when you consider aspects of life like traffic laws etc. but when it comes to God, where the whole point and aim is to love God and our neighbor, it is totally inadequate and counterproductive not to speak of insulting. How can you legislate for love? How can you compel love? How can you demand love under pain of punishment?

1 John 4. 'There is no fear in love, but perfect love drives out fear because fear has to do with punishment, and so one who fears is not yet perfect in love. We love because he first loved us.' Rom. 8. 'For you did not receive a spirit of slavery to fall back into fear, but you received a spirit of adoption, through which we cry, Abba, Father! The Spirit itself bears witness with our spirit that we are children of God, and if children, then heirs, heirs of God and joint heirs with Christ.'

In the secular world love is commonly downgraded to physical intercourse, or love of another's bank account or power or fame. But the love of which we speak here is appreciation, admiration, trust, mutual support, liking, friendship, steadfastness, honour, gratitude etc.

This is the love one hopes for from a marriage partner, from one's children, from one's friends and relatives. This is the love that God hopes for from his beloved children. It cannot be legislated or demanded or required or compelled. It is spontaneous, it is genuine, it is truth, it is persistent. So you can see how inappropriate it is to set up obligations when it comes to our relationship with our God. You can see how inappropriate it is for me to even think of obligation in my relationship with my God. Obligation under pain of censure poisons my relationship with my God just as it would poison my relationship with my marriage partner or my children. True religion (no matter which brand) is built on the realisation of what my God has done for me, and appreciation of God's goodness, faithfulness and love. This gives rise to a sense of gratitude to my God. Then all my religious practices (be it mass, prayer or sharing my good fortune with the needy) flow from this ever increasing sense of gratitude and hopefully (with God's help) will evolve into genuine love.

I have to be compelled to do it under pain of some punishment for non-compliance. For example I can only oblige you to run a marathon if you are not willing to do it freely. If you are willing and want to run a marathon I cannot oblige you to do it. The obligation fades away in the face of your willingness to do it.

So doing something because I am obliged to do it only proves that I do not really want to do it. Gratitude and love cannot exist under these circumstances.

4th Sunday of Easter (A) 2017

"I have come that they may have life and have it to the full." Like most of Scripture the above statement has meaning on a number of levels. Firstly it means that my life here on this physical earth is never full or complete. Can never be full and complete. All life here on earth can never be permanently sustainable. It is limited and circumscribed. It is fragile and changeable. Can swing from great to terrible. As the years go by it is subject to an ever greater need for healing. Permanent and definitive healing and fullness of life is not possible in this physical world. The life of Jesus of Nazareth was subject to the very same laws and restrictions during his whole life here on earth. For him fullness of life only came with death and resurrection. Permanent and definitive healing only came through death and resurrection into the Eternal Life of God. This is the gift he gave us. So too for you and I. Fullness of life, permanent and definitive healing will only come to us with death and resurrection into the eternal life of God. That is our destiny. That is why we were created and born. Secondly my life here on earth can have a certain direction and fullness or can be directionless and empty. Some young, unattached people, and not so young, unattached people can boast of their freedom. They can, up to a point, do what they like, when they like. But a time comes when this much vaunted freedom seems to pall, seems empty and pointless. There is something missing. It is only when their inward focused attention and self-centred concerns begin to look and focus outwards that life begins to bring a certain fullness. It is often when they commit themselves in love to another person and begin a family that their life begins to find fullness and meaning. The very sort of life they avoided in the past is the very thing which brings satisfaction, fullness and meaning to their life. So fullness of life is possible, up to a point, even here in this physical world. Strangely enough it comes, not from self-satisfaction but from selflessness. Not from acquisitiveness but from sharing. Not from freedom to do whatever I like whenever I like but from the freedom to serve the needs of others. Is this not embryonic Christianity? Is this not the first step in understanding the message of Jesus of Nazareth? Christianity is recognising all people as my immediate family - especially orphans and refugees. John 4. Jesus said to them. 'My food is to do the will of him who sent me.' John 6. Jesus said 'I came down from heaven not to do my own will but the will of the one who sent me.' How strange it is that even here on earth fullness of life only comes from looking after others, from service to others and not, as one would expect, from just looking after oneself.

5th Sunday of Easter (A) 2017

'Do not let your hearts be troubled. Trust in God; trust also in me.' The world contains great joy and great sorrow. There is great love and great hate. There is great health and great illness and pain. There is great hunger and great abundance. There is great good fortune and great misfortune. How does one reconcile this suffering with a totally good God. It is true that much of our suffering and pain results from one's own actions and words and much from the actions and words of other people. Even if I can blame myself or others for a lot of my suffering there still remains a lot of suffering which I cannot blame on anybody. So where does this leave me? It leaves me with the very same problem; Why does a totally good God allow suffering? Why did the Creator create a world where suffering is endemic? Over the years I have read everything I have come across on this subject. All are helpful to a greater or lesser degree on a theological and intellectual level. Not very useful on a practical, 'ad hoc', here and now situation. At this stage in my life I think that the answer must come from within, on two levels. Firstly, the person best qualified to bring comfort is one who has suffered the same type of pain or grief. One who actually feels the pain and grief of the sufferer. This ability is a precious gift to those who have actually suffered and grown with the experience, and should be recognised and used to bring comfort and acceptance to others. This is a ministry which many of you possess without realising it. Anyone of you who has undergone or are still undergoing, pain and grief, and still hold to your faith and trust in a totally good God, have a great potential to bring comfort and healing to those presently experiencing pain and grief. Not so much by what you can say to them but rather by your compassionate and understanding presence. By sharing in their pain and loss. Secondly the person them self who is suffering, must try and reach into them self and hold tight to their faith and trust in the total goodness of their God despite what they are going through now. For example; after Jesus was tempted for forty days in the wilderness and was exhausted, and again in the Garden of Gethsemane when he was overcome with dread of his approaching execution, we are told that angels came to comfort and strengthen him. Here, Angels can be taken as symbols, meaning that Jesus received comfort and strength from his total belief and trust in his God. It was his belief and trust in the total goodness of God and that his total wellbeing was safely in God's hands, that gave him comfort and strength to live through this pain, grief and distress. This is what I mean when I say that the answer to pain and grief must come from within. From within the comforter and the sufferer. It must come from my God who dwells within me. How else could the early Christians face or even contemplate being torn to pieces by wild animals in the colosseum for the amusement of the crowds. How else can a parent survive the death of a child and yet believe in a totally good God. How else can one survive the long drawn out pain and death of a lifelong marriage partner and yet trust in one's God. So when all is said and done we are left with the mystery of God and the apparent contradiction between perceived reality and the words of Jesus -'Do not let your hearts be troubled. Trust in God; trust also in me.'

6th Sunday of Easter (A) 2017

'If you love me, you will keep my commandments (my word, my teaching). And I will ask the Father, and he will give you another Advocate (Councillor, Paraclete) to be with you forever. This is the Spirit of truth, whom the world cannot receive, because it neither sees him nor knows him.' If you look for just one guiding influence in the life of Jesus of Nazareth it would be his adherence to what he believed to be the truth. The Bible is full of warnings against deceitfulness and lying. 'Proclaim the greatness of our God! A faithful God, without deceit, how just and upright he is."Keep your tongue from evil, your lips from speaking lies."Bread gained by deceit is sweet, but afterward the mouth will be full of gravel."Jesus then said to those Jews who believed in him. If you remain in my word, you will truly be my disciples and you will know the truth, and the truth will set you free."God is Spirit, and those who worship him must worship in Spirit and truth.' When I lie I spew the Spirit of God from my mouth together with my lying words. It is disgusting to listen to many of our so called leaders; political, civil and industrial, especially in recent years. We are fed on a diet of deceit and barefaced lies. Innocuously it is called spin but is deceit and lying and meant to cause confusion and misinform. When someone is brave enough to speak truth they are showered with ridicule and abuse. The world does not know, or want to know, Jesus of Nazareth, because they no longer want truth or to hear the truth. 'And this is the verdict, that the light came into the world, but people preferred darkness to light, because their works were evil. For everyone who does wicked things hates the light and does not come toward the light, so that his works might not be exposed. But whoever lives the truth comes to the light, so that his works may be clearly seen as done in God.' I cannot do much about the lying and deceitful ways of many of the leading figures of our various institutions but all of us can create an oasis of truthfulness around ourselves. This is lighting the lamp and placing it on the lamp-stand, 'where it gives light to all in the house.' Those who are honest with themselves will recognise the light of truth and will be affected by it. Our Pope Francis is a light on a lamp stand enlightening not only the Church but the whole world. Strangely enough the greatest opposition to the light he brings comes from within the Catholic Church itself. When we have something to hide we do not like the light. When our status and privileges are threatened we do not like the changes that truth may bring. The prince of darkness has many servants. Some willingly so, many not even aware of their slavery. 'Jesus said I am the light of the world. Whoever follows me will not walk in darkness, but will have the light of life.' For Jesus of Nazareth light, truth and fullness of life are one and indivisible.

Ascension (A) 2017

The instruction Jesus of Nazareth gave to his followers before he was executed was that they should go to Galilee where he would meet them again. Mtt. 'But after I have been raised up, I shall go before you to Galilee.' And the women who went to the tomb early on Sunday morning were told; Mtt. 'Do not be afraid. Go tell my brothers to go to Galilee, and there they will see me.' Why must the disciples of Jesus go to Galilee to see the Risen Lord? It was in Galilee, one of the poorest, most backward districts of Palestine, that Jesus of Nazareth exercised his ministry. It was here, among the poor and the dispossessed, that Jesus, we are told, went about doing good, healing the sick, sharing what he had with the hungry and speaking to them of the Good News of the Kingdom of God. So it was in Galilee that Jesus, the Risen Lord, gave his followers their mandate. This mandate was to continue the work he did in Galilee. His followers lived with him for a couple of years in Galilee, witnessing everything he did and said. Now their mandate was to continue this work until the end of time. They were to do this, not just on an individual level but as a community of His followers. This community or Church was the symbol of their being part of the community of God; the Father, Son and Holy Spirit. Being Baptised was a visible sign of their entry into the unity of this community or church. This community and the work it does is what Jesus of Nazareth called 'the Kingdom of God.' They would not be left to continue his ministry on their own. Just as he was physically present with them in Galilee as their mentor, exemplar and guide, so too now he would continue to be with them but not visibly so, except to the eyes of faith. So that is the mandate given to us, in our parish. As one community or church or parish we are to go about doing good, bringing healing to the sick and the grieving, feeding the hungry, and speaking of, and living according to, the Good News of the Kingdom of God.

Pentecost Sunday (A) 2017

Even a cursory examination of the Old Testament will tell you that it is a litany of failure. The repeated failure of the chosen people (the Israelites) to live as people created in the image and likeness of their Creator. Despite the many and repeated disasters which this failure brought upon them they continued on their self-destructive way. Through all this there was the 'remnant' who, to some extent remained faithful to the One True God. Though this 'remnant' had its ups and downs in their faithfulness to God, nevertheless, over and over again, they acted as a small nucleus around which the chosen people could coalesce in times of trouble and defeat. They acted as a beacon of hope to lead the people to the One True God when things were desperate. In the New Testament we see the same trend. The life of Jesus of Nazareth himself is peppered with disappointment, rejection, desertion in times of trouble and even outright betrayal by one of his closest followers. This trend continues today in the Body of Christ - the Church. We are the 'remnant' today. Despite our oft forgetfulness and our sometimes unfaithfulness to the One True God, yet we struggle (even if sometimes halfheartedly) to remain loyal to our God and Creator. We are that remnant; that beacon of hope, around whom the scattered people of God can gather and coalesce in troubled times or in their search for meaning and comfort in life. The fact that we are but a fraction of the population of this country or any country, this town or any town, should not bother us unduly. It was always so except where people were under pressure to comply. This is the gift of the Holy Spirit; that there is, was and always will be, the 'remnant,' who despite their many and repeated faults and failings, continue the struggle to be faithful to the One True God. To keep the memory of the One True God alive. Like the Israelites of the Old Testament, we the people of God of the New Testament are presented by our God with a daunting (one could say impossible) calling or vocation. In the Old Testament their calling was: 'You shall love the Lord, your God, with all your heart, with all your soul, and with all your mind. This is the greatest and the first commandment. The second is like it: You shall love your neighbour as yourself. The whole law and the prophets depend on these two commandments.' In the New Testament we are required 'to be perfect, just as your heavenly Father is perfect.' God my Creator is perfectly aware of my inability to live up to any of these callings. After all he made me and gave me these feet of clay. I can waste my time bewailing my present and past faults and failings, but that is not my vocation. While well aware of my feet of clay I keep my eye on the target. Like the athlete I strive to jump that bit higher or run that bit faster each day and disregard the limitations of yesterday. I refuse to be controlled by past events about which I can now do nothing. Being open to the Spirit of God who dwells within me, I take each day as an opportunity to live out my basically unachievable vocation, trusting in the wisdom of my God. As St. Paul said, 'God's power is made perfect in my weakness.'

Trinity Sunday (A) 2017

God so loved the world that He gave His only Son.

God did not send his Son into the world to condemn the world, but that the world might be saved through him.

God loves the world.

What does that mean?

God loves the stars. God loves the galaxies, the nebula, the black holes. God loves the clouds, the rain, the sunshine, the snow, the wind, the volcanoes and earthquakes. God loves the insects, the bacteria, the reptiles and the mammals, including human beings.

God created them as they are and loves them as they are. This degree of love is beyond my comprehension.

God's plan is the salvation of the world, be it astronomical singularities or great crested newts.

What does Salvation mean?

Salvation is the progression, over time, of primordial matter, by means of the Divinely installed evolutionary process, into self-awareness and an understanding of the Creator. Culminating in eventual union with the life and being of the Creator.

Why do we believe this?

We believe this because Jesus of Nazareth, who claimed to be God made man (the Creator) progressed from an initial one cell entity in his mother's womb through the various stages of the evolutionary process (again in his mother's womb) to be born as a human being. Growing in wisdom and understanding like the rest of humanity he accepted the trauma of death and burial but rose from the dead with a glorified body to rejoin the Holy Trinity from whom he originally progressed.

There were many witnesses to this, some of whom left us their witness in writing (the New Testament) and most of whom accepted death rather than deny what they had witnessed.

Today we celebrate the mystery of the Holy Trinity.

The Holy Trinity are the three separate persons who make up the One God.

Love (which we mentioned above) is the bond uniting the Three Persons of the Trinity.

True, genuine love is never inwardly focused. It is always outwardly focused. So the love of the Holy Trinity must be outwardly focused. Since, from the beginning, nothing existed but God the Holy Trinity was compelled to create other things so that their love could accomplish its compulsion to move or focus outwards.

So the reason for creation is God's love which of its very nature must encompass other things.

For the same reason we can say that nothing that God has created, or will create, will ever be discarded and cease to exist. All creation in some way must be gathered up into the life and being of the Creator - the Holy Trinity.

As St. Paul says in Rom: 8 ;

'We know that the whole creation has been groaning in labor pains until now; and not only the creation, but we ourselves, who have the first fruits of the Spirit, groan inwardly while we wait for adoption, the redemption of our bodies.'

What is our place in all this?

We are the only creatures on Earth (maybe in the whole universe) who can know and appreciate all of the above. We are the only ones who can consciously and overtly proclaim the greatness of the Creator and express our gratitude for existence and salvation. We are the focused voice of creation, able to proclaim gratitude and praise on behalf of all creation.

So let us lift up our hearts and give thanks to the Lord our God!

Corpus Christi (A) 2017

'Behold, the virgin shall be with child and bear a son, and they shall name him Emmanuel, which means God is with us.'

'Behold, I am with you always, until the end of the age.'

The great desire of my God is that I believe and recognise that God is with me. This is the message of the Bible.

This is why God the Son, the second person of the Holy Trinity, became a human being and lived and died among us.

God made Man; Jesus of Nazareth, demonstrated to me, by word and example, that his sole concern is my total welfare. My God wants me to have a long, happy and healthy life here on earth before joining Him in Eternal Life.

The world will try and convince me that happiness is getting plastered drunk on Friday night and making a total ass of myself.

The Eucharist; Holy Communion, is the great symbol of Emmanuel. The visible and tangible sign of my God's presence with me and in me.

Holy Communion - the Eucharist, the Mass - is not given to me so that I can spend time in adoration. It is to remind me that Jesus of Nazareth is with me and in me so that I may go forth and live as he did in Galilee, showing compassion, tolerance and forgiveness, sharing my good fortune with, and helping my fellow human beings, as and when I can.

A big problem with me is my ability to spend time before the Blessed Sacrament and then go forth as intolerant, unforgiving, selfish, nasty and mean as when I came in.

The latter is comedy; it is a big joke.

So receiving Holy Communion is not about spending a short time in prayer and adoration but about going forth and living as Jesus of Nazareth lived.

'For as often as you eat this bread and drink the cup, you proclaim the death of the Lord until he comes.'

A second aspect of Holy Communion, of the Eucharist, is remembering.

Remembering that on Holy Thursday evening just before his arrest, he celebrated the Last Supper with his Apostles and instructed them to do this in memory of him. This is the Mass, the Eucharist.

So when I receive Holy Communion I remember. I remember not only the Last Supper but also the Passion, execution, burial, and Resurrection of Jesus of Nazareth.

I look on the Crucifix and ask myself, can I trust one who is willing to undergo such an ordeal on my behalf?

12th Sunday of the Year (A) 2017

In today's Gospel reading Jesus of Nazareth tells his Apostles that they are to proclaim his message openly and completely. The instructions he gave them privately as his closest group and the explanations he gave them on many occasions are not just for them but to be proclaimed to the whole world - 'what you hear whispered, proclaim on the housetops.'

They must not be afraid. Even if you are threatened with torture and even death because you are Christians - fear not. God, whom you serve, is more powerful than any and all who threaten you.

Trust in your God at all times and in all situations, for your total wellbeing is your God's main concern. After all the sparrows are counted and cared for as are the hairs on your head (few or many as they may be!). I must not try to conceal my belief in God or what I believe to be right and wrong, especially in a world that ridicules morality and belief in God.

13th Sunday of the Year (A) 2017

'Whoever loves father or mother more than me is not worthy of me, and whoever loves son or daughter more than me is not worthy of me.'

Here we are talking about 'amoral familism.' That is the extreme type of family bond which existed in Palestine and still exists, even today, in some cultures. For example 'honour killing of a member of a family to preserve the honour of the family.' Willingness to do extreme hurt to any outsider who threatened the family in any way.

What Jesus of Nazareth is telling his disciples is that even if your family disapprove of your being a Christian or do not want you to live as a Christian, this must not deter you from following Jesus of Nazareth.

Situations like this are common today when only one member of a family is Christian or when a son or daughter might wish to enter the religious life.

'Whoever gives only a cup of cold water to one of these little ones to drink, amen, I say to you, they will surely not lose their reward.'

What about the ones who install and maintain a water supply for a whole town?

What about those who build and maintain roads and transport systems?

What about those who build and maintain property?

What about those who educate and guide our children?

Those who look after our mental and physical health?

The ones who keep our money safe and administer it wisely and honestly?

Those who keep the peace so that we can live safely in our homes?

Those who remove our rubbish and waste? etc. etc.

In all these things it is the motivation and the dedication that matters.

I can give a cup of cold water to a thirsty person just to get rid of them or because I really want to help them, as a person; as a brother or sister.

I can repair a person's car as fast as possible and as cheaply as possible just so that I get my money, or I can do it conscientiously and carefully so that the owner can travel safely and dependably.

In everything I do the personal element must be involved. What I am doing is for somebody, will help somebody, is important to somebody and that somebody is a very valuable, a very important person because he/she is a child of God and my brother or sister. If one is looking after a home; washing, cleaning, ironing, cooking etc., getting the motivation right is much easier if it is for people you love and respect.

That is why Jesus did not just say 'Whoever gives only a cup of cold water to one of these little ones to drink, amen, I say to you, they will surely not lose their reward.'

What He said was; 'whoever gives even a cup of cold water to one of these little ones in the name of a disciple, truly I tell you they will not lose their reward.'

Here understand 'in the name of a disciple' or 'because they are a disciple,' to mean, because they are God's children and your brothers and sisters.

This is the motivation which can give the most repetitive and boring tasks meaning, at least some of the time.

This is what can sanctify the work I do. This is how I can 'pray always without becoming weary,' and fulfill St. Paul's exhortation to 'pray at every opportunity in the Spirit.'

My work; Everything I do and say can evolve into a prayer. In this way there will be no distinction, no separation, between work, prayer and leisure.

14th Sunday of the Year (A)
2017

We are always being urged to pray. The following are my ideas on prayer.

If I were to follow the regime of prayer which I was required to follow in the seminary and which was expected of me for the rest of my life as a priest I would spend four hours each day in prayer.

If I were living a monastic life where prayer was the only focus of my day then that is ok. As a parish priest working with and among people it is totally unrealistic.

Naturally, I and most other secular priests, had to abandon many, if not all, of these spiritual exercises.

We were taught that there were spiritual things or activities and profane things or activities. (Here, profane means secular, not religious, not related to God.)

Anything which was not prayer in the strict understanding of the word (for example being on your knees in church or reciting the rosary or the psalms etc.) was profane.

Even preparing people for the Sacraments and administering them could be regarded as profane and draining on our spiritual resources.

This had, and still has, a profound effect on our relationship with our God.

To keep in contact with God one had to stop doing profane things and get on ones knees to top up one's spiritual batteries with 'real' prayer.

This way of thinking and acting was unrealistic for secular priests (that is Diocesan Priests) but far more so for lay people.

I would even say that it had, and still has disastrous consequences for our relationship with our God. We end up thinking that there are parts of our life which involve God and most of our daily life has nothing to do with God.

The truth is that God is involved in every aspect of our lives. The truth is that everything we do and say and think can be as much a prayer and involve our God as when we are celebrating Mass or praying on our knees.

Gen. 'God saw all he had made and indeed it was very good.'

Rom. ; 'I know and am convinced in the Lord Jesus that nothing is unclean in itself.' It is my attitude or intention which makes something profane.

Nothing is objectively unclean. It is I who make something unclean.

I am not saying that I should not spend some time in traditional prayer. On the contrary I am saying that I can spend all my day in prayer with a little effort and forethought.

For most of us, life is an adventure of discovery. An adventure of discovery in the company of my marriage partner, my children and my grandchildren. Throughout the day my thoughts keep returning to them in one way or another, irrespective of how busy or preoccupied I am.

What I am trying to say is that if I can include my God in this family bundle; Then, I and my God worry about them. I and my God hope they are ok. I and my God look forward to meeting them in the evenings or after school or during supper together. I and my God getting them bedded down for the night. I and my God up and about to prepare breakfast and get them all off to school or to work. I and my God planning our family holiday together etc. etc. With a little effort and practice this togetherness with my God can easily extend to those I work with and meet casually during my day. In this way my whole day is a prayer. In this way my whole day or most of it is spent in the company of my God.

Formal prayer has its place in my life but only as part of my everyday life and work, which is my real prayer.

If I confine my contact with my God to the times of formal prayer then I will not be spending much time with my God.

15TH SUNDAY OF THE YEAR (A) 2017

My earliest memories of my dad are mind pictures of him immersed in his vegetable garden. These would be the second world war years. All his life he fed his family from his garden and any surplus went to neighbours and friends.

All his life he would come home from work and go directly to his garden. He wasn't into flowers. Everything he grew was for the table.

Weeding was a continuous, unrelenting, task which was always part of my life. It was a never ending war. I learnt to munch cabbage, carrots, turnips and peas as I weeded.

He died in February. The afternoon before he died suddenly of a heart attack he was out in his garden planning the programme for the spring planting.

I have no doubt that Joseph and Mary had a vegetable garden also and that the young Jesus was constantly pressed into the task of weeding etc.

So he knew what he was talking about when he told today's parable.

Planting and nurturing the seeds of faith; of belief in God; of gratitude to God our Creator, has always been and always will be a challenge, a puzzle, a conundrum.

My experience over the years is that one can give any given group of persons, who declare interest in joining the church, exactly the same teaching, exactly the same preparation, exactly the same process; Some will drop out during the process, some will drift away after reception into the church and some will continue as convinced and dedicated members.

This seems to be normal.

Jesus said to them. 'It is the spirit that gives life, while the flesh is of no avail. The words I have spoken to you are spirit and life......But there are some of you who do not believe.... For this reason I have told you that no one can come to me unless it is granted him by my Father. As a result of this, many of his disciples returned to their former way of life and no longer accompanied him.'

So the parable of planting the seed of God's Word on all types of soil is the best way to describe the work of the catechist. What happens then is up to the Father and He is keeping it close to his chest.

Why this is so? Your guess is as good as mine.

Ours not to reason why, Ours but to do and die.

16th Sunday of the Year (A) 2017

Probably the most devastating trait of any religion is the urge to control, the urge to dominate, the urge to power.

This urge is almost ubiquitous in one way or another in human politics, in human societies, even in the human family.

Christianity is the antithesis of this.

'For the Son of Man did not come to be served but to serve and to give his life as a ransom for many.'

'At that time the disciples approached Jesus and said, Who is the greatest in the kingdom of heaven? He called a child over, placed it in their midst, and said, Amen I say to you whoever humbles himself like this child is the greatest in the kingdom of heaven.'

The greatest among you must be your servant. Whoever exalts himself will be humbled; but whoever humbles himself will be exalted.'

'Jesus sat down, called the Twelve, and said to them, If anyone wishes to be first, he shall be the last of all and the servant of all.'

'Jesus said, the one who is least among all of you is the one who is the greatest.'

Most, if not all religions, including ourselves, have conveniently forgotten this. We shower each other with titles and fancy costumes to denote our importance and our greatness. We seem incapable of freeing ourselves from our addiction to greatness and recognition.

Do we Christians ever think of this as a fault, as a sin? Surely this involves the first two of what used to be called the seven deadly sins - pride and covetousness!

When Jesus said 'Why do you notice the splinter in your brother's eye, but do not perceive the wooden beam in your own eye?' surely this was one of the things he had in mind. Religions so often condemn sexual misdemeanours and totally ignore their own lust for power, control and influence.

Many of our clergy are antagonistic to the reforms which Pope Francis is trying to bring about. They fully realise that what he is trying to do will challenge their power, their dignity, their control - their greatness. He calls it clericalism and severely condemns it. Parish priests are certainly not immune to the above.

All of us in our parish must be aware of, and avoid, any desire to praise ourselves or our achievements. We must avoid trumpeting our praises to others. Self praise is always suspect. What Jesus said as regards almsgiving is also applicable here - 'Do not let your left hand know what your right is doing
And your Father who sees in secret will repay you.'

17TH SUNDAY OF THE YEAR (A) 2017

Again today Jesus of Nazareth is trying to get across to me what the Kingdom of Heaven is. What it is like.

Imagine the Kingdom of God or the Kingdom of Heaven as a very happily married couple who are comfortably well off with one child. They appreciate how blessed and lucky they are and want to share this blessedness and good fortune with others, both people and things. They adopt a child and another and another. They get a dog and a cat and maybe a canary.

They look after and share their good fortune with all these things. They love all these things and treat them as their own, as their family. They make provision in their will for all their family.

The kingdom of God always existed. Everything that ever existed, that exists now and that will exist in the future is part of the Kingdom of God. In other words the whole of creation belongs in the Kingdom of God.

This fact was not known and was not knowable to creation until evolution produced human beings who were sentient and self aware. Then God became a human being called Jesus of Nazareth who made us aware of the Kingdom of God. Who make us aware that we and the whole of creation were part of God's family and were loved and cherished by God as such.

Our lives and the whole of creation were no longer encompassed by the words birth, life and death. Rather I should think of my existence as firstly; conception/creation.

Secondly; physical, mental and spiritual growth and understanding. Thirdly; Glorification into the consciously visible, tactile and experiential reality of the Kingdom of God.

The Kingdom of God or the Kingdom of Heaven (which are one and the same thing) is mentioned 93 times in the New Testament.

I often think of death as the gateway into the Kingdom of God. This is not so. I already live in the Kingdom of God. What I call death is gaining the ability to see, hear, touch and experience, first hand, the Kingdom of God. My present body (a product of the evolutionary process) must be discarded and replaced with a glorified body. (To quote Jesus of Nazareth: Truly, I tell you, unless a grain of wheat falls into the earth and dies, it remains just a single grain; but if it dies, it bears much fruit.') Only then can I see, hear, touch and experience the reality in which I already live - the Kingdom of God.

Speaking in metaphor Jesus described the latter as follows; 'In my Father's house there are many dwelling places. If there were not, would I have told you that I am going to prepare a place for you? .... I will come back again and take you to myself, so that where I am you also may be.'

What we call death is the arrival of Jesus of Nazareth to take me to his Father's house.

And St. Paul tells us; What no eye has seen, nor ear heard, nor the human heart conceived, what God has prepared for those who love him.'

> The above may give me some degree of comfort, of acceptance, when my thoughts turn to death, as they inevitably do. As time passes, it may somewhat lessen my sense of loss and grief at the death of a loved one. We are all in, and part of, the Kingdom of God - those of us who already see and hear and those of us who are awaiting the opening of our eyes and ears.

Transfiguration (18th Sunday of the Year) (A) 2017

I have read the gospel of the eighteenth Sunday rather than that of the Transfiguration because it seems to me to be so relevant to our situation today.

I think that we dodge the bullet when we say that the feeding of the five thousand is a prefiguration of the Eucharist where we are all fed spiritually with the Bread of Life.

To my mind Jesus sees the many people in front of him. He sees that they are physically hungry and thirsty. His disciples' attitude mirrors my reaction and maybe yours; 'Send them away so that they may go into the surrounding country and villages and buy something for themselves to eat.' It sidesteps the questions as to whether food is available for buying and do they have the money to buy it.

Jesus simply tells them; 'You give them something to eat.'

For me the message of today's Gospel reading is that the example of Jesus and his disciples sharing the little they had with those nearest to them was the catalyst which prompted others to share what they had brought along with them with those who had forgotten to bring anything or had nothing to bring.

We are told, 'They all ate and were satisfied.'

Surely our own experience is that when we get together and share there is not only enough to go around but some left over.

FATHER JOHN

In the Gospel reading for the Feast of the Transfiguration a voice from the bright cloud (God the Father) tells us; 'This is my beloved Son. Listen to him.'

The glaring need today; The obvious need which we are all dodging and sidestepping - what this generation will be condemned for by future generations - is our attitude towards and treatment of migrants and refugees be they political or economic. The shame of the years of slavery will be compared with what we are allowing to happen today.

Be totally sure that if Jesus of Nazareth were here today he would be found on the shore of the Mediterranean or Aegean sea rescuing migrants from the water or urging Governments to accept and care for refugees.

We are inclined to brand those brave and selfless enough to go to the help of refugees and migrants as partly responsible for encouraging the migrants. Even some of our political leaders suggest that they be left to drown to discourage others. How unchristian can we be?

> I console myself that I am doing my little bit while secretly aware that I could and should do much, much more.
>
> We console ourselves as a Parish that we are doing our little bit while secretly aware that we could and should do much, much more.
>
> I must listen to Jesus of Nazareth telling me, 'You give them something to eat.' And the voice of the Father telling me, 'This is my beloved Son. Listen to him.'
>
> Do I want to lie on my death bed bitterly regretting how little I did to help my brothers and sisters in dire need?

19TH SUNDAY OF THE YEAR (A) 2017

Depending on your understanding of the Bible, today's reading can be taken as a factual account of what actually happened or as a symbolic narrative or parable to give the Christians of that time courage in their trials and to strengthen their faith.

At the time of writing this narrative the Church (the boat) was being persecuted and Christians executed and scattered (buffeted by the waves and wind).

Despite their plight Jesus was with them (Jesus went out to them, walking on the water).

They were terrified and cried out in fear but Jesus said to them: 'take courage! It is I. Don't be afraid.'

The ambiguity of their faith is graphically demonstrated by the actions of Peter; brash overconfidence immediately followed by fear and doubt.

The message is clear: 'You of little faith, why did you doubt'.

For a generation now the boat (the Church) has been buffeted by the winds and the waves. Scandals have multiplied. Church leadership has been found wanting or totally lacking. Many have abandoned the Church. Vocations to the priesthood and religious life have fallen dramatically. Up to recently, efforts at rejuvenation have been confined to regression to the certainties of the past.

Today a new spirit is slowly filtering into the life of our church. A spirit of freedom, co-operation, mutual respect and appreciation of each others talents.

In the Old Testament we read, time and time again, how the Israelites (the chosen people) wandered from belief in the One True God and his teaching and how this was closely followed by defeat and disaster. These defeats and disasters were interpreted as punishments from God for their faithlessness.

We know that Our God does not punish us, his children. It is we who, when we abandon faith in our God and wallow in selfishness, greed, exploitation, national and tribal interests, to the detriment of unity, generosity, mutual respect and sharing of the gifts Our God has given us, allow injustice and oppression to creep in and become the norm. It is this situation, which we ourselves bring about, that causes wars, economic disasters, financial collapse, deprivation and hunger.

Our Church's troubles, recent and present, are the direct results of the very same causes which we (our Church) have brought upon ourselves. For too long our church has concentrated on control of the member, political influence and preserving the good name of the institution at all costs to the detriment of the total wellbeing of the members.

The buffeting of the winds and the waves which our church has and is experiencing are the direct result of our own waywardness.

But Jesus of Nazareth is calling out to us 'take courage! It is I. Don't be afraid.'

> We must let Jesus climb back into our boat (into our church, into our parish, into our hearts). Only then will the wind die down and the calm of total trust in our God abide in our hearts, our parish and our church.
>
> So now is a time of great opportunity for our church and our parish and for each one of us. We have learned, the hard way (the only way), that seeking influence, control, power and blind obedience are not God's way.

We have learned that power corrupts and our church is no exception. I must now cultivate an open and gentle heart, a receptive and welcoming parish and a church which is of service to all God's children.

20th Sunday of the Year (A) 2017

The Four Gospels seem to differ slightly in their understanding of who Jesus of Nazareth was.

You will remember the questions Jesus asked his Apostles; Who do people say I am?" and "Who do you say I am?"

The answer to this question was hotly debated in the early church. It was only finally settled in 325 AD at the Council of Nicaea where the Nicene Creed was produced, (which you all have on your mass cards.)

A side issue to this central question was how much did Jesus of Nazareth know and understand about himself and when did he know and understand it.

The Synoptic Gospels (Matthew, Mark and Luke) seem to give us good grounds for thinking that Jesus grew in understanding of who he was and what his mission was as he grew physically and mentally - just like you and I.

On the other hand the Gospel of John seems to indicate that from the very beginning of his life Jesus of Nazareth fully understood who he was and what his mission was and exactly how it would unfold.

Today's Gospel reading is a case in point.

If you hold that Jesus knew and understood everything from the very beginning, that he was sent to bring salvation to all mankind irrespective of ethnicity, then why refuse to help the Canaanite woman because she was not a Jew?

On the other hand if you hold that Jesus grew in wisdom and understanding through out his life, as we read in Luke "And Jesus advanced in wisdom and age and favour before God and man," then we can see that this was what was happening in today's reading. We see Jesus beginning to understand that God's promises were not just for the Chosen People-the Jews-but for all peoples, Jews and Gentiles.

Now, the interplay between Jesus and the Canaanite woman in today's Gospel reading makes sense. It shows his growing understanding that faith is not the province of the Jews only but is found in, and belongs to, all peoples.

This question of the admission or exclusion of the Gentile races was a major problem for the first century of the Church's existence. Peter and Paul had a big confrontation on the question which was the subject of the first general council of the Church.

It is interesting that it is the pleading of a suffering mother fearful for the welfare of her child and her obvious faith in God, that brings Jesus to his senses and a fuller understanding of his mission.

Last Tuesday was the feast of the Assumption of Our Blessed Lady (Mary) into heaven.

> Devotion to Mary is found from the earliest days of the church. I can only guess at the distress and grief of a mother witnessing the torture and slow execution of her child. I can only guess at the distress and grief of a mother receiving the dead body of her child in her arms and having to bury it far from home. No wonder we should, and do, cry out to Mary in our distress and grief.

21st Sunday of the Year (A)
2017

All religions seem to demand/require/suggest a certain approach to God.

All religions try and figure out what God is like and from their conclusions tell us what God wants from us - how God wants us to treat Him. This approach colours our liturgical practices and official prayer life.

This is why different religions honour God and pray to God in many differing ways.

For example St. Patrick's Missionary Society decided at the beginning to follow the spirituality of St Ignatius of Loyola (St. Ignatius, the founder of the Jesuits, invented/instituted this approach).

This approach to God suited some but not many.

The problem I find with all of the above is its presumption that, irrespective of who I am, it requires me to approach and treat God in a certain way. I can see the value of this approach as a starter, but having started (after a number of years) I should allow the Spirit of God to lead me in my relationship with My God.

God is a Person. Religion is a relationship with this Person. Like all personal relationships it must grow, develop, change, mature.

Adhering closely to a certain form or practice of religion in our relationship with God can for some be good and very helpful depending on the character, makeup and needs of that person. For many it can impede ones personal relationship with ones God. One can lock one-self into a stylised and rigid form of worship which treats God as an object of worship. This can be far removed from a personal, warm, grateful, appreciative relationship with ones God.

For example take a learned Biography of Nelson Mandela written by someone who has read all that is written about him and interviewed people who knew him but has never actually met or spoken with him, and contrast it with the personal understanding and memories of someone who knew him well, spoke regularly with him, was imprisoned with him for years.

In the former you know about the person (second hand knowledge) in the latter you actually know the person and have a personal relationship with him.

That is why some of our church leaders are obsessed with form, correct doctrine, unchanging formulas and closely regulated liturgy. For them God is an object to be worshipped with the correct words and actions but they have not met God personally. They know much about God but do not know God as a person. That is the big difference between Pope Francis and those who oppose him.

This highlights what I have mentioned to you over the years; the ongoing tension within our Church (and within all religions) between Law and Prophesy. Between going by the book and risking change. Between staying in the boat and stepping out onto the water.

God loves all his children unconditionally whether they stay safely in the boat or trust in God and venture out onto the waves. But if I want to really know my God I must hold his hand and to reach him I must walk on the water.

So the question for me personally is: "But what about you. Who do you say I am."

22nd Sunday of the Year (A)
2017

It was obvious to Jesus of Nazareth, as it was to his Disciples, that because of his lifestyle his opposition to and his preaching against, oppression, injustice and intolerance, that if he went to Jerusalem (the seat of power of his enemies) for the feast of the Passover, he would almost certainly be arrested and imprisoned or executed.

Jesus well understood that he could run and hide from his enemies but not without being untrue to his preaching and example. He could save his life but not without losing his credibility. He could run but only at the cost of vitiating his message and the power of his example.

At this particular time Peter and the Apostles did not understand this way of thinking. They could only see the looming danger and try to avoid it irrespective.

Having slapped down this approach pretty smartly, Jesus proceeded to explain why and what his point of view was.

What follows is all about freedom. The freedom of the children of God. The words free and freedom appear many times in the New Testament.

What is the freedom of the children of God?

It is the freedom to do the right thing. It is the freedom to do good. It is the freedom to love. It is the freedom to forgive. It is the freedom to give things away. It is the freedom to do the will of the Father.

FAITH... IS A JOURNEY

To quote Jesus of Nazareth in John 8;

'I do nothing on my own, but I say only what the Father taught me.... I always do what is pleasing to him....If you remain in my word, you will truly be my disciples and you will know the truth, and the truth will set you free.'

If he selfishly gave in to his Apostles importuning to run and hide he would save his life but would lose credibility and his message would be forgotten and lost. Hence his words, "whoever wishes to save his life will lose it." But if he remains true to his calling and to his preaching, if he wants his message to be noted and preserved, then he must go to Jerusalem for the feast and accept the consequences, "those who lose their life (for my sake) will find it." The best way I can explain this is to tell you a true story about one person in South Africa. Khandy was a young catholic lady who came to mass from time to time. She was about twenty or twenty one and had finished her secondary education two or three years before. She had been trying to get accepted into a nearby teachers training college - so far unsuccessfully. A couple of years later she succeeded and eventually emerged as a trained teacher. The next few years were spent trying to get a teaching position in a school. Eventually in her late twenties she got the job. Then about a month later she arrived in to see me. She handed me a fat A5 size envelope. I was a bit nonplussed, so I opened the envelope to see what it contained. It was full of Rand notes to the value of about eighty pounds. I asked what this was for and she said it was an offering to the church. At my obvious confusion she explained that when she was trying to get a place in the teacher's training college she promised God that if she succeeded and got a job she would give half her first month's salary as an offering of gratitude to God. I was totally gobsmacked. Not because of the amount of money but because I knew that up to now she had been totally dependent on her parents handouts and must for years have longed for her own money so that she could buy some of the things she so much desired. Despite her promise to God it must have taken an extraordinary degree of self-denial to give away, to lose, half her first month's salary. I am sure that if her parents or peers knew what she had done they would be scandalised and regard her as a fool. At that moment she was truly free. Free to do what she understood to be the right thing. Free from the slavery to money.

I still remember what she did. I even remember her name, when so many others have faded from my memory. Many of you too will remember what she did.

And what about God? Will her God not remember that supreme act of selfless freedom for all eternity?

Am I free? If someone suggested that I was not free I would bridle indignantly.

A simple test will tell me the truth. I know that if I were to give half of next months income to some worthy cause it would be a very good thing and would not greatly affect my financial situation. But am I free to do it? Try it and see.

That is what today's Gospel reading is about.

Of course the presumption is that, to quote Jesus of Nazareth, 'when you give alms, do not let your left hand know what your right is doing.'

27TH SUNDAY OF THE YEAR (A) 2017

The one thing which always angered Jesus of Nazareth was hypocrisy.

Whether it came from the chief priests, scribes, pharisees or his own apostles and followers, he roundly and directly rejected it.

It included refusal to accept the truth which is staring one in the face, for selfish reasons, such as greed, fear of losing control and power or loss of 'face.'

Although today's Gospel reading is directed towards the Jewish religious leadership of the day it is as easily applicable to the religious leadership of today.

Even in the last fifty years many of God's servants, both clerical and lay, sent by God to remind the tenants of the vineyard, that it was not theirs to do with as they pleased and that they owed the owner his proper share of the harvest, have been expelled from the vineyard (the Church) and metaphorically stoned.

We today (both clergy and laity) have to shed our hypocrisy also. Looking deeply into my heart I must ask myself are my prayers and devotions, declaring my love and gratitude to God, authentic and true, or merely compliance, and a covering of my posterior? Are my declarations of undying loyalty to my God largely motivated by fear and a desire to 'gain' a place in heaven, or avoid 'hell'? Is our failure to inspire our children, grandchildren and friends with an appreciation of the goodness and love of our God, the result of the lack of such appreciation, gratitude and love in my own dealings with God?

This is hard for me and you to accept.

Far from wishing to condemn, we must accept the fact that in this matter we have largely failed.

But as Jesus of Nazareth said; "The truth will set you free." Free to recognise my hypocrisy, discard it, and move forward to a proper relationship with my God, based on understanding, gratitude and a total trust in the goodness of God, no matter what situation I find myself in.

This is true religion. This is authentic religion. Anything else is counterfeit and will immediately be recognised as such by our children, grandchildren and friends.

I for one, have for many years lived a false religion and a false God.

No wonder so many have rejected our religion and our God.

My aim is not for us to look back in guilt, or allow ourselves to become disheartened, discouraged or depressed. Rather that we should rejoice that we are now beginning to understand our past hypocrisy and are moving towards a good relationship with the true God. A God who is happy, joyful, compassionate, forgiving and totally good.

Pope Francis is today gently removing from the vineyard (from church leadership) the original tenants and trying to replace them with tenants who will give God his rightful share of the harvest.

This is sparking great opposition and protests just as it did in Jesus' time.

So in our Faith, in our Church, in our parish, in our lives, let us move forward together, with joy in our hearts and a total trust in our God, for whom 'all things are possible.'

28TH SUNDAY OF THE YEAR (A) 2017

'Behold, I have prepared my banquet, my calves and fattened cattle are killed, and everything is ready; come to the feast.'

I want you to note the sense of urgency.

How many of us have prepared a meal and when everything is just ready we call the family or the guests to the table. How many of us have felt the frustration of our family or guests delaying for some trivial reason while the plates and the soup gets cold.

We want them to come now not in five or ten minutes time.

The Lord has prepared a great banquet for us. When all is ready God calls us to come to the table to eat and drink. The invitation is for now. Everything is ready, come now.

Like in today's parable a decision is required. I must choose to come now; not tomorrow or next week or next year. Now is the time.

This is conversion. This is saying yes, now, to the Kingdom of God, to the Reign of God in my life.

From this moment on I seek to do the right thing, to act justly, to forgive generously, to share with joy. To live in, and as part of, God's Kingdom.

For Jesus of Nazareth the Kingdom of God was not something for the future but an already existing reality.

'Asked by the Pharisees when the kingdom of God would come, he said in reply, 'behold, the kingdom of God is among you.'

For Jesus of Nazareth the Kingdom of God had already been inaugurated, had already begun.

His cures and miracles were signs of the already presence of the Kingdom of God; that the power of God had already taken over from the power of evil.

'Others, to test him, asked him for a sign from heaven. 'He replied, 'if it is by the finger of God that I drive out demons, then the kingdom of God has come upon you.'

And again at Cana when water was changed into good wine we are told; 'Jesus did this as the beginning of his signs in Cana in Galilee' (signs that the Kingdom of God had arrived) 'and so revealed his glory, and his disciples began to believe in him'

The Eucharist itself guarantees that we already occupy the Kingdom of God. Receiving Holy Communion is the sign, the confirmation, that I am one with Christ. United with Jesus of Nazareth in the Eucharist I already 'sit at the right hand of the Father' in the Kingdom of God.

So for me Christianity, religion, must mean living up to what I already am - a resident of the Kingdom of God - and not about striving to gain something in the future.

As Jesus of Nazareth said. 'Behold the Kingdom of God is among you.'

You might well say; 'But I don't feel as if I am already in the Kingdom of God! In my pain or grief I feel far from God and far from God's Kingdom!'

Then again neither did Jesus of Nazareth, as he struggled to carry the cross on the road to Calvary. Or as he died in agony on the cross and shouted out 'My God, My God, why have you forsaken me?'

So religion for me is an act of gratitude. A deep sense of thanks for this great gift which I have already received - the banquet in the Kingdom of God.

29th Sunday of the Year (A) 2017

After listening to the parable about the invitees refusing to come to the wedding feast, which we read last weekend, the chief priests, Scribes and Pharisees were livid because it meant that they had rejected God.

So they upped the ante.

The question about paying tax to Caesar was a very political and sensitive one. To say no was treason as far as the Romans, the Herodians and all civil servants were concerned and would result in immediate arrest and execution. To say yes was totally unacceptable and unpatriotic to the Jewish people who regarded the Roman tax as unjust and as a symbol of their oppression by foreigners.

Cannily enough the Pharisees did not ask the question themselves as this might put them under suspicion by the Romans, so they sent some of their disciples (the less bright ones) to ask the question publicly. In today's political jargon they wanted 'plausible deniability.'

They seemingly had Jesus between a rock and a hard place.

The denarius, was a roman coin used to pay the tax and was regarded as the symbol of the oppression of the Jewish people. It was hated and reviled. It also figured the head of the Roman Emperor and alluded to him as divine.

So Jesus' reply - 'repay to Caesar what belongs to Caesar and to God what belongs to God' -neatly outflanked the problem.

It indicated that (as every Jew believed) everything belongs to God and should be given to God, while the only thing which belonged to Caesar was this hated coin with his head and name on it - the symbol of oppression - which every Jew would gladly give back to Caesar, together with his reign of oppression.

We should take note of the total opposition of Jesus of Nazareth to oppression of any kind. There are the obvious cases of the oppression of one nation by another or of one ethnic group by another. There are also the less obvious cases of the oppression involved in human trafficking and exploitation of the weak.

Nearer to home there is the oppression exercised in the workplace such as bullying and the belittling of others and of their efforts. Lastly there is the oppression exercised in the home, in the family.

If I am honest with myself I will easily distinguish between necessary discipline in the family and needless or deliberate oppression and bullying.

One is good and necessary for a happy family environment while the other is hurtful and brings unhappiness and division.

We have all experienced enjoying a happy gathering of family or friends. Then another person joins the group. Suddenly the whole atmosphere changes. Conversation peters out, every word is carefully chosen before being spoken. Everyone is 'tiptoeing on eggshells.' The atmosphere becomes oppressive.

Also vice versa. A very stilted and oppressive meal or party changes immediately when one or two persons leave. The whole atmosphere becomes convivial and free flowing.

This is something we can all examine our consciences about. I can oppress another deliberately or I may also act oppressively without being fully aware of it.

Sitting down occasionally, and prayerfully and honestly examining my day, both at work and in my family, and the relationship I have with each person therein may reveal some unpleasant facts about me which need attention. This exercise can be far better for my spiritual welfare and my relationship with others and with my God, than just an enumeration of 'sins' committed.

30th Sunday of the Year (A)
2017

Just look around you. Almost all our troubles are the result of ignoring the one reason for, and the basic aim of, all being, all existence, all life.

"You shall love the Lord your God with all your heart, and with all your soul, and with all your mind. This is the greatest and first commandment."

It is totally outgoing. It is totally encompassing. It is totally fulfilling.

Why is this the greatest of the commandments?

God - the Creator, is the source of all existence. God is the beginning and the end of all creation. Everything comes from God and returns to God. Outside of God nothing exists or can exist.

This commandment or teaching or instruction is not God being selfish or self-centred. It is a simple fact of existence. It cannot be otherwise. It is simply the truth.

To 'love the Lord my God with all my heart' is not about feelings and emotions which come and go - are here today and gone tomorrow (although these can sometimes be involved). Nor is it about praying and other cultic acts and devotions (again, these can sometimes be involved).

To 'love the Lord my God with all my heart' is primarily an act of humility. A recognition of the truth - that all I am and have is a free gift from my Creator. Whether I like it or not I owe God everything.

It means that I owe all the works of God's hand - all of creation - the very same care and respect which I expect for myself. This must not only involve respect and care for myself but also for my family, friends, neighbours, fellow human beings, all living things, the seas, the mountains the lands the forests and everything they contain. This, involving truth and the way things are, is the only way to permanent peace, happiness and contentment at the deepest level. Seeking these things outside of these parameters brings only fleeting peace and momentary happiness.

It involves an ongoing struggle to comprehend God and creation while recognising and accepting human inability to fully understand or explain the whys and wherefores of creation. It is not really possible for human beings to love an invisible, untouchable, incomprehensible, infinite God. We love God by respecting, appreciating and caring for his creation - fellow human beings and all things animate and inanimate.

Hence the second command (instruction), is like the first; 'You shall love your neighbour as yourself.'

Is it really possible for me to love my God and be unaware of - ignore - the suffering of His children?

Is it really possible for me to love my God and ignore the devastation His creation is being subjected to all over the world?

This is what true religion is primarily about.

I am inclined to, and often encouraged to, immerse myself in prayer and various devotions and cultic acts of worship, while sidestepping the real meaning of loving God and my neighbour.

I wouldn't like the words of Jesus of Nazareth, spoken to the Scribes and Pharisees, to be applied to me also : 'Woe to you, Scribes and Pharisees, hypocrites ! For you tithe mint, dill and cumin, and have neglected the weightier matters of the law – justice and mercy and faith. It is these you ought to have practiced without neglecting the others. You blind guides! You strain out a gnat but swallow a camel !

The Feast of All Souls (A)
2017

When and where I grew up, All Souls Day was inextricably linked with a place called Purgatory.

Purgatory projected one image only; all our deceased relatives, friends and acquaintances crying out to me for release from the agony of the fires of Purgatory, which was said to be the same as Hell but of shorter duration. I, through prayer, fasting and almsgiving could shorten their period in Purgatory. Causing myself to suffer for their sake was said to be particularly efficacious.

If people were lucky enough to escape the eternal fires of Hell they, almost in every case, had to do long stints in the fires of Purgatory to be cleansed of their guilt. Depending on their sinfulness, this period in Purgatory could be from mere days to many years.

All the above was aimed at coercing people into obeying the church through the fear of punishment. There is no evidence for such teaching. It is an invention of misguided teachers.

If God could do the above then I want absolutely nothing to do with such a God.

That is why, up to now, and only at the request of parishioners, have I agreed to celebrate All Souls Day as a separate event. For me All Souls today and All Saints, yesterday, is about one and the very same people.

To quote Jesus of Nazareth; 'And this is the will of him who sent me, that I should lose nothing of all that he has given me, but raise it up on the last day.'

And again on the Cross to one of the murdering thieves; 'Truly I tell you, today you will be with me in Paradise.' Today, not tomorrow or next week or next year. Nothing about time spent in Purgatory for cleansing from past sins. Today you will be with me in paradise.' It was now 3.00pm and the Jewish day ended at 6.00pm.

Today I agree to celebrate All Souls day not so that I can help them but to remember them and to rejoice that they are with God and can help me.

To even suggest that my God is anything like what I was brought up to believe is insulting to my God and insulting to me, a son of God.

So today we fondly remember all our deceased relatives, friends and fellow parishioners. We thank them for the privilege of having known them. For the help they gave us. And having completed their lives here on earth and received the gift of Eternal Life with our God, we congratulate them and ask for their help in our journey through this life.

Finally we look forward to meeting them again in Eternal Life where everything will be known, understood and forgiven.

31ST SUNDAY OF THE YEAR (A) 2017

One of the hardest things for any human organisation is to avoid a power structure. Even among the Apostles we see it creeping in.

Then James and John, ... came to Jesus and said to him. Teacher, we want you to ... grant that in your kingdom we may sit one at your right and the other at your left.'

This was problematic among the Apostles and is so to this day in our church.

It is problematic in all churches and all religions. Even those christian churches who abolished bishops and priests have replaced them with different power structures.

Like the exhortation to love God and our neighbour (which we explored last weekend), today's exhortation to avoid power structures among the followers of Jesus of Nazareth has been sidestepped with exceeding nimbleness.

In fact religions are structured like armies (uniforms and all) with the emphasis on obedience to the next layer of the structure.

In our church this situation is found not only among the clergy but also among the so called laity.

If I ring up a parish asking to speak to Pat Murphy I will get the frigid response from the parish secretary, 'hold on and I will put 'the Very Rev. Canon Patrick Murphy' on the phone. One finds oneself forced into this power structure. Today's Gospel reading is not saying that it is wrong to call one's

Rabbi; Rabbi, or one's father; father, or one's mother; mother, or one's teacher; teacher, or one's priest; father; or one's bishop; bishop. What is wrong is the attachment of power or superiority to the title. This leads to pride, an overbearing attitude to others and a subservient attitude in others.

Jesus of Nazareth was at pains to teach his followers by example and by words;

'For who is greater: the one seated at table or the one who serves? Is it not the one seated at table? Yet I am among you as the one who serves.'

'So when he had washed their feet and put his garments back on and reclined at table again, he said to them. Do you realise what I have done for you? You call me teacher and master, and rightly so, for indeed I am. If I, therefore, the master and teacher, have washed your feet, you ought to wash one another's feet. I have given you a model to follow, so that as I have done for you, you should also do.'

Then he sat down, called the Twelve, and said to them, anyone wishes to be first, he shall be the last of all and the servant of all.'

"You know that those who are recognised as rulers over the Gentiles lord it over them, and their great ones make their authority over them felt. But it shall not be so among you. Rather, let the greatest among you be as the youngest, and the leader as the servant.' Isaiah, prophesying in the Old Testament about the Messianic era to come said; "Remember not the events of the past, the things of long ago consider not; See, I am doing something new! Now it springs forth, do you not perceive it? In the desert I make a way, in the wasteland, rivers."

Jesus of Nazareth wanted his followers (his church) to be something completely new. Something free from the curse of power structure. This will not come from the top. It must begin and be implemented at parish level. Only we can do it.

Not only do we 'so called' clergy need to change our superior attitude in a power structured church but also you, 'so called' laity, need to change your subservient attitude towards the clergy.

Pope Francis has told Vatican officials and the bishops of the world to cease and desist from naming members of the clergy to be canons and monseigneurs.

We will see if this instruction is followed.

32nd Sunday of the Year (A) 2017

This well known story is an allegory or a symbol or parable which has to be interpreted. It is intended for the followers of Jesus of Nazareth. That is for people who declare themselves to be Christian.

With the expectation of the imminent return of Jesus (the last day) fading, some of the Christians (though still professed Christians) were slackening off in their adherence to Christian values and practices (something we are all familiar with today).

The parable is a reminder that, even though we trust and hope in our God's mercy and compassion as regards our Eternal Salvation, we have no absolute certainty as to what will happen (just as we have no absolute certainty as regards the existence of God). So the message from today's parable is to look to the future and to be prepared for whatever happens.

The oil for the lamps stands for good works - love God and your neighbour. It pertains to the person themselves and is not a transferable asset.

The final sentence is the message for me today; 'Therefore keep watch, because you do not know the day or the hour."

33rd Sunday of the Year (A) 2017

Last Sunday and next Sunday the theme is the same. Do not slacken off or grow weary, keep up the good work realising that whatever I do as regards my fellow human beings, be it good or bad, I do to my God.

The above is the message as we come to the end of the liturgical year (the church's year).

The threat of punishment from our God for non compliance, at the end of these three gospel readings is not the message.

The message is, do not grow weary or get disheartened but be alert and prepared and live our lives in faith, hope and total trust in our God no matter what.

To use our God given talents to the best of our ability for our own good and the welfare of others.

To constantly reminding myself that, how I treat other human beings (and other creatures) is how I treat my God.

The threats of punishment at the end of each reading are human editorial inserts and not from our God or else need a deeper understanding and interpretation of scripture than we have today.

This is obviously so because we know that our God wants our response to him to be freely given - to be one of sincere love, gratitude and respect. This is impossible if there is a threat of punishment involved for non compliance.

This becomes even more obvious if you take your own case. How satisfied and happy would you be if you had to keep your children and grandchildren in order by threats of punishment or exclusion from your will? Surely the threat involved would at least damage if not destroy any hope of genuine love and gratitude.

God is no fool and would not queer the pitch for himself even before the game starts.

Feast of Christ the King (A) 2017

Every day, from the moment I wake up in the morning until I fall asleep at night, is a judgment on me – I continually make little or big choices throughout my day. Each choice makes me a better or worse person. Each choice makes me more human or less human. Each choice contributes to the sort of person I turn out to be.

Today's Gospel reading is not about what will happen at the end of the world. It is not about God dividing the 'good' from the 'bad'. It is not even about God passing judgment.

It is a very graphic story about what living as a human being, created in God's image and likeness, is, or is not.

There is no talk about religious affiliation or theological understanding.

These things; religion, scripture, theology, motivate me, encourage me, help me, constantly remind me so that I may make the right choices throughout my day.

What are these choices?

"I was hungry and you gave me food, I was thirsty and you gave me drink, a stranger and you welcomed me." Or. "I was hungry and you gave me no food, I was thirsty and you gave me no drink, a stranger and you gave me no welcome."

This is my judgment. My daily choices are my judge and my judgment.

Not when I die. Not at the end of the world.

Every hour of every day is my judgment.

Every choice I make or don't make is my judgment.

The personal choices I make every day are what brings peace and joy to my life or come back to haunt and trouble me in the future.

When someone stands to give the eulogy at my funeral what would I like to hear said and what would I not like to hear said?

Now, today, is the time to do the sort of thing I would like to hear said.

The sort of thing for which I would like to be remembered.

'Fight to the death for truth, and the Lord God will fight for you.'

'Above all pray to the Most High that he may direct your way in truth.'

'Most important of all, pray to God to set your feet in the path of truth.

'God is Spirit, and those who worship him must worship in Spirit and truth.'

(I tried to count the number of times 'truth' is mentioned in the Bible. When I got to 170 I gave up counting.)

It is well known that a confession made under duress or torture is not credible.

Therefore if you believe that if you do not give food to the hungry, if you do not give clothes to the naked, if you do not welcome the stranger etc. you will be condemned to 'the eternal fire,' then what credence can be given to the sincerity, the truth, of whatever you do.

It is a sham and the god who requires me to act under such coercion and threat is also a sham.

So whatever the source of and the meaning of the threats we find here and there in the Bible, still remains to be worked out in the future, but we can be sure that their source cannot be the God who desires worship in spirit and in truth.

1st Sunday of Advent (B) 2017

Today, the First Sunday of Advent - the beginning of the Church's new year.

For those sensitive to the liturgy it is year B for Sundays and year 2 for weekdays. Advent is a time of preparation.

A time of preparation for the Lord's second coming and for the anniversary of the Lord's first coming on Christmas day.

Last Sunday we examined the idea of the Last Day and Judgement - the Lord's Second Coming.

We examined the idea that each one of us is his/her own judge. That our judgment is what each of us do or don't do; what each one of us is or is not.

We have no idea about what Eternal Life will be like. It will not just be life that goes on and on. It will be a sharing in the life of our God and our Creator.

One thing we can be sure of is that sharing in the life of God involves the following, and I quote; 'We have come to know and to believe in the love God has for us. God is love, and whoever remains in love remains in God and God in them.'

So, how can I share in the life of God if I hold enmity or hatred, or anger or jealousy towards another person - towards one of God's beloved children? How can I meet my neighbour in Eternal life if I am still seeking revenge on him/her?

How is this to be ironed out (if it can be ironed out)?; your guess is as good as mine.

One thing for sure; I cannot live in union with God in eternal life if there are people around who I refuse to meet or talk to.

This is what Jesus of Nazareth is talking about when he told us;

'if you bring your gift to the altar, and there recall that your brother has anything against you, leave your gift there at the altar, go first and be reconciled with your brother, and then come and offer your gift.

Settle with your opponent quickly while on the way to court with him. Otherwise your opponent will hand you over to the judge, and the judge will hand you over to the guard, and you will be thrown into prison.

Amen, I say to you, you will not be released until you have paid the last penny.' The above are graphic stories or examples of what I need to do now.

Some time ago I visited a person who was dying. He knew he was dying. He was content to die. He felt at peace with his God. I brought up the name of a person with whom I knew he was at enmity, hoping that, at least in his own mind, there was some reconciliation. He immediately flared up in anger towards that person. The next day he died, I hear peacefully! Seeing as our God has given us free will and respects our free will, I often wonder what God can do in cases like that, which are many.

Back to Advent. The time for preparation, not Just for Christmas, but also for our entry into Eternal Life.

Why not think of this Advent as being 'on my way to court with my opponent.' This is my opportunity to settle with my opponent - to seek reconciliation, to offer reconciliation, to seek healing for hurts given and received, to try and realise that, as in my own life, many ways I react and act are the result of my upbringing, environment and genes. So too for other people. Realising and accepting that we are all wounded in one way or another, be it physically, psychologically or spiritually, can help me to be tolerant, forgiving and understanding.

'You have been told, 0 man, what is good, and what the Lord requires of you: Only to do right and to love goodness, and to walk humbly with your God.'

Advent is a good time to try and walk with my God.

2ND SUNDAY OF ADVENT (B)
2017

"Behold, I am sending my messenger ahead of you; he will prepare your way."

John the Baptist was called by God to prepare the people of Israel for Jesus of Nazareth. Firstly John preached repentance.

There are different kinds of repentance.

True repentance has nothing to do with fear; fear of God, fear of Hell, fear of punishment, fear of embarrassment, fear of discovery.

True repentance is a deep regret for hurt, pain and injury which I have directly caused to others or am in some way implicated in.

For example, I can be directly abusive to others or I can vote for someone I know is abusive to others. I can steal myself or I can buy something I know or strongly suspect has been stolen. I can dent someone's parked car and drive away unnoticed or I can leave a note with my phone number.

The test is truth. Am I truly repentant for hurts or injury I have caused directly or indirectly or am I repentant because of some perceived repercussions for myself.

For years and years I went to confession seeking forgiveness, but my motivation was not true repentance but selfish self preservation from future perceived punishment. What is now known as 'covering one's ass.'

That is why I question how the sacrament of Reconciliation has been presented to us and is still presented to us. It fosters self interest, self preservation. It is not authentic. It is focused on oneself and the protecting of oneself from future unpleasant repercussions and retribution. There are exceptions of course and some people do demonstrate true and deep repentance for hurts given and help withheld.

But I believe that by and large Confession, as still practised today, is counterproductive, unauthentic and largely self deception. I would recommend that each one of us looks back over the many times we have gone to confession over the years and judge honestly for oneself.

My aim is not to cause you to worry about the past and whether you have been forgiven or not. Forget about the past. Trust in one's God and look to an authentic future where you walk hand in hand with your God.

My God does not want me to wallow in regret, guilt or have scruples about the past. These are detrimental to my relationship with my God and stultify my spiritual life.

My God wants me to plant the flowers of justice, love, compassion and giving in the garden of my life and not waste my time continually trying to uproot weeds.

3rd Sunday of Advent (B) 2017

John 1:26-27.
"There is one among you whom you do not recognise."
Is this not my big problem as a Christian? My refusal or inability to recognise Jesus of Nazareth.
Is this not my God's biggest headache?
God has been revealing Himself; has been present among us, since the beginning of time, through the works of His hands - through creation.
God has been revealing himself; has been present among us, through his Word, in Scripture, for two to three thousand years.
God has revealed himself to us by being born, living and dying, just like us, in the person of Jesus of Nazareth.
God has told me that He lives in me and I live in Him, on many occasions.
God has told me that he is the vine and I am the branch.
God has told me that "I am with you always, until the end of the age."
God has told me that whatever I do for, or to, anyone of my fellow human beings, I do to God Himself
You could go on and on in this vein.
And yet my biggest problem as a Christian is recognising my God who is always in my presence, who lives in me, in whom I live and move and have my being.
But I keep putting my God at a distance, on a pedestal, up in the clouds. The present language used in the Mass and in

other liturgical cerebrations does not help. Here we address our God in subservient, servile, and even grovelling language. We address our God using imperial and royal modes of address.

The God we treat in this way is the God who told us that when we address him we should begin 'Abba" meaning 'daddy.'

The God who told us 'the one who is least among all of you is the one who is the greatest.' The God who 'when he had washed their feet...said to them. 'Do you realise what I have done for you? You call me teacher and master, and rightly so, for indeed I am. If I, therefore, the master and teacher, have washed your feet, you ought to wash one another's feet. I have given you a model to follow, so that as I have done for you, you should also do.'

So why do we treat our God as the majestic emperor living far off in unattainable light. That is exactly what God told us not to do, yet our liturgical language is full of it.

No wonder I keep my God at a distance. All my God wants is to hug me to his/her breast. The Christmas lesson is 'Immanuel' meaning 'God with us.'

That is why today is called 'Gaudete Sunday.' Gaudete means let us rejoice.

We rejoice today - and every day- because our God is always with us.

4TH SUNDAY OF ADVENT (B) 2017

The most important sentence for me in today's Gospel reading is the very last one. Mary said yes.

'Then the angel departed from her.'

God is a smooth operator. He sent Gabriel to this young girl, barely out of her teens. He came with fine words of praise and great promises for the future. When Mary broached a small problem - she wasn't married - it was answered with high sounding words of reassurance. No mention of her becoming a pregnant unmarried woman (the penalty for this was death by stoning) or that her boyfriend would want to break of their relationship as a result. No mention that she would have to solve this problem on her own with apparently no Angelic help. And this was only the beginning of her troubles; No mention of the early death of her husband and that she would have to cope on her own. No mention of the arrest and execution of her son as a common criminal.

This resonates with me. I became a priest on a flood tide of optimism about the importance of the calling, the great work awaiting to be done and the dignity and sanctity of priesthood in the sight of God and man. I didn't pause to consider any drawbacks.

I said yes.

Then the angel departed from me.'

That is how God works.

God created me and Mary and you with certain and differing abilities. He coaxes us into saying yes. Then he disappears and lets us get on with it using the abilities God has given us. The gift of free will demands that things be so. It demands the freedom to love or not love, the freedom to choose good or evil, the freedom to build up or to knock down.

I am sure that Mary woke up in the morning from time to time wondering how on earth she got herself into such a position.

I have awoken in the morning from time to time and wondered what on earth I am doing in this job.

Without doubt, you also have woken up in the morning, from time to time and wondered how on earth you ended up as you are.

But of course the Angel does not depart.

God does not depart.

It is only looking back over the years that one can appreciate that God did not depart.

It is not only the abilities and strengths which God gave me that have helped me, but also many things I regarded as my weaknesses can now be seen as protections from danger and harm.

'Behold I am with you always. Yes, to the end of time.'

It is through struggle, hard work and failure, that I grow, mature and increase in wisdom and understanding.

Christmas is our guarantee of God's constant presence, guidance and help. Immanuel. Success in life has nothing to do with one's salary, one's possessions, one's health, one's standing in life.

Success in life is about conscious living in the presence of one's God. Immanuel.

Christmas (B) 2017

All creation is a revelation of what God is like, through the work of God's hands.

The Bible is a revelation of what God is like through the writings of various people who were inspired to write down what their understanding of God was.

The Incarnation - the birth of Jesus of Nazareth at Christmas - is a revelation to us, in the person of Jesus of Nazareth, of what God is like.

At Christmas we remember and celebrate the birth of Jesus of Nazareth.

Because of the coming of Jesus of Nazareth we no longer have to wonder about God - what he is like or how He would act in certain circumstances.

Now we can learn all about God from looking at and listening to Jesus of Nazareth.

From what I can see, when there is dispute about what God wants or doesn't want, about what is right or wrong, it boils down to human reluctance to accept the truth. It boils down to self interest, greed, avarice. It boils down to a refusal to forgive, to tolerate differences, to share, to help those in need.

In prison, John the Baptist had the same problem. He was having doubts as to who Jesus of Nazareth really was so he sent some of his friends to ask Jesus himself.

The reply they got was : "Go and tell John what you have seen and heard: the blind receive their sight, the lame walk, the lepers are cleansed, the deaf hear, the dead are raised, the poor have the good news brought to them. And blessed is anyone who takes no offence at me.

John the Baptist, and all of Israel, were looking forward to a Redeemer who would be like King David. One who would scatter and destroy all the enemies of Israel and set up a powerful and independent nation.

But Jesus of Nazareth was speaking and practising, mercy and forgiveness, healing of the sick and the grieving, unity and sharing, love and compassion and not vengeance, nor destruction of perceived enemies, not war and scattering, not suspicion and marginalisation.

John the Baptist and all of Israel found this hard to take. They had been brought up on their nationalism, on their superiority as a people, on their exclusivity. Vengeance for past wrongs and revenge on their enemies was a holy grail. That is why many would take offence at what Jesus of Nazareth did and said. (Would not many of us today, take offence also, in today's context.)

Jesus of Nazareth would have none of this.

We are told: "God anointed Jesus of Nazareth with the holy Spirit and power. He went about doing good and healing all those oppressed by the devil, for God was with him."

Christmas is about healing, co-operation, unified action, tolerance of differing attitudes, cultures and beliefs. So, don't just think about having a 'merry' Christmas. Think about having a tolerant, forgiving, unifying Christmas.

Epiphany (B) 2018

If you like you can take the story of the coming of the Magi as symbolic rather than historical.

For the Jews the Magi would be strange people - pagans who knew nothing of the God of Israel or the Scriptures. Seekers of truth and wisdom through astronomy, astrology, mathematics and other, to the Jews of that time, mysterious sciences.

For the authors of the New Testament they symbolised the coming of peoples from all nations to belief in, and worship of, Jesus of Nazareth; the Messiah.

These authors would have been very conscious of the prophesies concerning the Messiah as found in Psalm 71 and in Isaiah 60 which speaks of dignitaries or kings coming from afar bringing gifts to the Messiah.

It is disputed as to whether some strangers actually came from afar following some astronomical event (which were widely associated with the birth of a king or emperor) or that the authors of Matthew simply put it in as a suitable fulfillment of Old Testament Prophesy. Either way doesn't really matter as the aim is not historical fact but theological instruction.

For me there are two lessons in today's Gospel reading which stand out.

Firstly it is of great importance to be a seeker of truth. My natural attitude should be, to quote Einstein "The more I learn, the more I realise how much I don't know." The Magi travelled a long distance seeking the truth, not fearing what the truth might reveal but ready to accept the truth and change if necessary. Science is the seeking of truth. I have heard many times 'I do not believe in a God, I am into science.' Such a one understands neither science nor theology. A great thing about science is that it will debunk false theology. Good theology will always dovetail with good science.

If there is an apparent contradiction then either science or theology must reappraise their conclusions.

The second lesson from today's Gospel reading is that truth will not always be welcomed.

King Herod and the political establishment of the day did not want truth. (their response to truth was to kill it).

The religious establishment did not want truth - they already knew it all (they didn't even bother to send someone to Bethlehem to look into the matter.)

Primarily Christianity is a seeking of truth - truth about God and about man.

Even in today's allegedly 'enlightened' world, anyone who openly professes their religious belief and especially tries to live by it, will encounter ridicule and even persecution of one sort or another. It can often go under the label of 'peer pressure' and can be found even in our own schools and homes. Being a Christian requires one to be morally and mentally strong.

As regards the gifts which the Magi brought, one mum remarked 'typical men. It never occurred to them to bring nappies.'

2ND SUNDAY OF THE YEAR (B) 2018

Look, the Lamb of God!'
They followed Jesus.'
What do you want?
Where are you staying?'
'Come and you will see.'
They spent that day with him.'

When John the Baptist spoke of the one who was to come and then pointed him out, John's many followers were naturally curious.

Today we see how two of them became followers of Jesus of Nazareth.

This pattern was probably followed by many others.

They do not seem to have been persuaded by theological arguments, quotations from scripture or miraculous works. They were curious, they saw how he lived and heard what he said and were convinced.

We have the very same when John the Baptist (now in prison) had doubts about Jesus from reports he heard. Jesus told the people John sent to question him, `Go and tell John what you hear and see.'

This seems to be the pattern that Jesus followed; People heard about him from others. They were curious. They came to him, they saw and heard and became his followers.

What Pope Francis is trying to do - what our own Bishop is trying to do with the new three year programme, 'A people of

Hope' and 'A future full of Hope,' is to persuade us to come to Jesus of Nazareth so that we can see and hear.

As you well know Jesus of Nazareth is no longer visibly present.

Jesus of Nazareth is present today in his followers. in groups of people who are dedicated to living in accordance with the example and the word of Jesus of Nazareth.

'Behold, I am with you always, until the end of the age' he told his followers.

So if people want to see and hear Jesus of Nazareth they have to do so by looking at us and listening to us. That is by looking at and listening to those groups of people who claim to be followers of Jesus of Nazareth. That includes us - the people of our parish.

So to put it in a nutshell, what Pope Francis is trying to do and our Bishop is trying to do, is to persuade our church to be a place where people can come to hear Jesus of Nazareth and to see how Jesus of Nazareth lives. Unfortunately for you and I this cannot be achieved by simply reforming our church's hierarchy. It must involve a personal conversion for you and I. We can have a brilliant Vatican leadership and administration, a brilliant Diocesan leadership and administration but if I and you do not reflect the life and teachings of Jesus of Nazareth in our church and in our lives, it is to no avail. We must make it possible for people to come to our parish and there see and hear Jesus of Nazareth.

How just one of us acts, what just one of us says, the attitude of just one of us is what attracts a person to Jesus of Nazareth or puts them off. So each one of us is directly responsible as to whether people can see and hear Jesus of Nazareth in our Church in our parish, or not. This is called evangelisation.

3rd Sunday of the Year (B) 2018

Jesus of Nazareth did not come to start a new religion.
He did not come to bring us new doctrine.
He came to bring us 'Good News.'
What is 'good news.'?

(Imagine you are in a dead end job. You and your family are struggling to make ends meet. You constantly fear eviction from your house because of arrears in rent. Then you get an official letter from an attorney in America informing you that a far off relative, of whom you have never heard, has died leaving three million dollars. After a long search you are found to be the nearest living relative. After costs you are due two million dollars and sixty five cents.)

This will certainly qualify as good news. This will certainly change your life. It will involve a change in attitude.

(Imagine you are diagnosed with cancer. Tests suggest it is very aggressive with a very poor prognosis. You are operated on with little hope of success. Post operatively you are informed that it is not as aggressive as feared and was successfully removed in its entirety and there is no reason why you should not live to a ripe old age.)

This will certainly qualify as good news. This will change your life. This will involve a change in attitude.

What 'Good News' did Jesus of Nazareth bring me?

For me the Good News is that we are all God's children. We are all brothers and sisters. My Creator is intimately involved in every aspect of my life. My God is totally committed to my physical and spiritual wellbeing.

This situation is not and cannot be merited, achieved, gained, or earned in any way, no matter what I do. It is pure gift. Given freely with no strings attached. The only input I have is to accept the free gift or reject it.

I think that this is great news.

This Good News has the added perk of involving resurrection from death and sharing Eternal Life with God.

To be authentic the motivation for all religion must be gratitude.

Unfortunately religion is often presented as the way to merit or gain or win Eternal Life. This is false religion and is insulting to God.

All theology and Scripture must be interpreted in the light of the above facts. If theology, doctrine, or scripture does not seem to fit in with the above then these discrepancies must be reappraised and reinterpreted.

Basically prayer must be contemplation of, thinking about, these gifts from God so that our hearts might overflow with gratitude.

Irrespective of what my life is like, the very fact that I live, have being, exist, am conscious of myself and of things around me is, in itself a fantastic gift.

4th Sunday of the Year (B) 2018

Today I continue with what I said last weekend.

Jesus of Nazareth was sent by the Father to bring us 'Good News'.

The Good News is that I am a child of God. God is intimately involved in my everyday life.

God is totally dedicated to my physical and spiritual welfare. As a child of God I will inherit the Kingdom of my Father. This involves resurrection from death and sharing in the Eternal life of my God.

This is good news.

But that is not all. All the above is a free gift. It is not necessary to win or merit or gain it is a gift given to, or offered to, every human being by the Creator, with no strings attached. Like every gift (big or small) it can be accepted or rejected by the intended receiver.

This is the teaching of Christianity. This is the Good News brought to us, from the Father, by Jesus of Nazareth. It is crystal clear. It is transparent. It is straightforward. It is unambiguous.

Today we speak about acceptance or rejection of the Good News. We speak of my response to this Good News. Whether I accept or reject the Good news, the consequences for me are basically unknown and unknowable in any detail.

At this stage we find that what is crystal clear and transparent becomes muddied and opaque. This is the result of human imagination and casuistry. Human beings, be they the authors of Scripture or theologians, try to second guess God. A typical example is the idea of Heaven and Hell. We human beings demand reward for what we consider as doing good and punishment for what we consider as doing bad. We transfer or attribute our own attitudes and biases to God. This is called anthropomorphism. Another example is the attributing to God, in the Bible, of the characteristics and outlook of medieval monarchs and rulers. Hence eternal life with God if you obey Him and the fires of hell if you disobey him. This is all very understandable concerning us human beings but must not be attributed to Our God.

If you want to cling on to the idea of heaven and hell as places of reward or punishment then at least try to understand it as accepting or deliberately rejecting a precious gift.

God is totally free. Because we are made in the image and likeness of God we too share in this freedom. This demands that we have choice. We can accept or reject.

Recently there is a lot of talk about robots especially human like robots or androids. Imagine a marriage partner who is an android. There would be total obedience, total compliance, total dependability. There would be no rows, no inconsistencies, no surprises, no resistance, no compassion, no concern, no love.

God does not want androids. God wants the hurly burly of human relationships. The joy and sorrow of love and rejection. The heat and cold of human interaction.

If I exercise God's gift of free will to accept God's gifts then I am using the gift which God gave me. If I exercise the gift of free will to reject God's gift then I am also using the gift which God gave me. So why should God punish me for using his gift of free will?

> I hope I have given you some idea of the futility of trying to second guess God. Once we leave the crystal clear waters of the 'Good News' we just stir up mud and have no idea where we place our feet.

So I recommend that rather than wondering about and questioning the ins and outs of the Good News (Which will only leave you as wise about it as you are now) we concentrate on our response to the Good News. This is the heart of the matter. This is what religion is about.

This again is very simple and crystal clear. It is what my normal, everyday, natural response to any gift is - gratitude. Gratitude gives birth to respect, appreciation and affection which can grow into love. And who knows what delights love will lead to.

5th Sunday of the year (B)
2018

"For by grace you have been saved through faith, and this is not from you; it is the gift of God; it is not from works, so no one may boast."

This means that salvation is not and cannot be a reward for good works.

Catholic teaching is that faith or justification or salvation is a free gift from God. Catholic teaching also requires good works for salvation.

This does not mean that by good works I can merit or gain or win eternal salvation.

Faith is a free gift from God. By faith in God I realise and believe in the many gifts which God my Creator has freely given me. I am free to accept or reject these free gifts. Believing in and accepting these free gifts will inevitably bring about a response from me. This response can only be gratitude. Gratitude naturally gives rise to respect and liking. This will naturally lead me to seek to please the giver of the gifts. This seeking to please the giver of the gifts leads to what we call good works. Therefore in this sense only do we understand the phrase 'faith and good works are necessary for salvation.'

It is a natural progression. They are part of one and the same thing.

This understanding is widely overlooked, but it is a huge and all important difference. Consider the following carefully;

1) I believe in God and in the free gifts of God. I understand and accept these free gifts. Out of gratitude to God for his goodness and generosity I strive to please God in every way I can.
2) I believe in God and the gifts of God. I want these gifts very badly. I believe that I have to obey God if I want to gain these gifts. My motivation is self interest. I am in constant fear that I will offend God and thus lose these gifts.

The first is the 'Good News of great joy for all the people' brought to us by Jesus of Nazareth. The second is the Old Testament belief and understanding of God.

The key here is a sense of gratitude. Gratitude to my God for His many free gifts.

To feel gratitude to someone I must have an understanding of what that person has done for me. I must regularly remind myself of, and think about, what that person has done for me. I must fan this flame of gratitude in my heart until it becomes the principle motivation in my life. This constant recalling of and increasing understanding of God's free gifts to me must be the principle ingredient of all my prayer. Surely this was why Jesus 'went off to a solitary place, where he prayed.'

All the above is just common sense. Something we are all aware of in our everyday relationships with people. Do you want your marriage partner and your children to like you and enjoy your company or do you want them to fear and obey you? Do you want your friends to accompany you on your holiday because they enjoy your company or because they are hoping that you will pay for them? Do you want to receive Christmas gifts because of the gratitude the givers feel towards you or because they are expecting much greater gifts in return? You be the judge.

Our weekly Mass is all about gratitude for gifts received.

It recounts to us, it reminds us - we God's family here in our parish - of God's many gifts to us and expresses our gratitude, in an official and symbolic way. It is the act, the official act, not of individuals, but of a whole congregation together.

This is expressed together as a congregation when, led by the presider (the Priest), we all respond with one voice at the beginning of the canon of the Mass; The Lord be with you. And with your spirit. Lift up your hearts. We lift them up to the Lord. Let us give thanks to the Lord our God. It is right and just.

In all things relating to God and religion it is not what I do that matters. It is why I do it.

6TH SUNDAY OF THE YEAR (B)
2018

I did mention last weekend that the Mass is the official, and symbolic act of gratitude, of God's family in a particular area.

I also mentioned that down the centuries this official act of thanksgiving has accumulated various additives and accretions. The latter did have meaning and relevance at the time. However this relevance faded with time but the accretion remained. (For example the official opening of parliament, while being colourful, is for most people largely unintelligible). The power of symbols tends to be lost as time passes. Then new relevant symbols are needed but rarely initiated.

'The original Mass was simply a meal of bread and wine shared together in someone's home. The sort of meal shared with family and friends.

This shared meal was in direct response to the meal of bread and wine shared by Jesus of Nazareth and his disciples on Holy Thursday evening just before his arrest and execution. After this meal he asked them to do this in memory of him.

This memory of him is, that he was sent by the Father to bring us the Good News and all that this entails (as we saw for the last few weeks). This memory includes God's total commitment to my welfare even if it requires the ultimate sacrifice - execution on a cross.

So Mass is remembering what God has done for me and us and saying thank you. This shared meal expresses our unity as God's family here in our parish and our shared sense of gratitude.

This is simple, straightforward, crystal clear and effective. Or should be.

Some of the historical and outdated accretions were removed after Vatican II but quite a few still remain. These continue to obscure the essential nucleus of the Mass which is a simple shared meal.

Of course we human beings, both laity and clergy, become attached to our out of date, historical, and now irrelevant customs. Down the centuries laws and regulations are formulated as to the clothes that must be worn, what the bread must be like, what strength the wine must be, approved suppliers, what the make up of the candles must be, what the Ash Wednesday ashes must be like and how produced, Mass vessels, altar cloths etc etc must be this way and that way.

What the Mass is and what it is about gets lost in the dense vegetation and verbiage. How much more out of touch can one get than having a get together meal with your family and insisting that you speak in Latin throughout the meal; a language which none of them know!!

For the time being we are more or less stuck with what we have as regards the Mass.

The trick is to train oneself to see through all the shrubbery and recognise the simple meal of bread and wine shared together in grateful remembrance of our God's goodness to us.

1st Sunday of Lent (B) 2018

The first part of today's Gospel reading is totally symbolic in nature.

I paraphrase it.

Soon after his nomination by John the Baptist as The One Who Was To Come,' Jesus needed to think and pray about this new calling. So he went off by himself for a while.

He was well aware of the dangers attached to this calling and the many enemies he would make.

He was sorely tempted to just forget about it and disappear back to Nazareth and the quiet life there. But he realised that if he did that he would forever be plagued with regrets and guilt for failing to respond to God's calling. So trusting in God's goodness and help he made his decision and went back to join John the Baptist at the Jordan.

The second part of today's Gospel reading is a very brief synopsis of the public life and teachings of Jesus of Nazareth.

Soon after John was arrested and imprisoned, Jesus went to Galilee (his home province). There he spent most of the rest of his short life moving about in the towns and villages doing good and speaking of the Kingdom of God.

If I do not grasp something of the meaning and reality of the Kingdom of God then I have missed what Christ's coming and his message is about.

The Kingdom of God is here. I am in the Kingdom of God. Those yet to be born, we now alive on this earth, and those gone before us into Eternal Life, are all part of the one reality - the Kingdom of God. Call it God's family, call it the Mystical

Body of Christ, call it Eternal Life, call it the Communion of Saints, call it the Holy Trinity family, call it the Life of God. In the Kingdom of God we are all brothers and sisters. In the Kingdom of God there is no Jew or Gentile, no black or white or brown, no male or female. All are Gods children sharing in God's Eternal Life. The Kingdom of God is God looking with delight on his beloved children, all different, all loved, all cherished.

The same is true for the whole of creation. All things, great and small, belong to the Kingdom of God.

The message, the invitation, is to live out our lives here on earth as members of, as part of, the Kingdom of God.

Why not let our parish be the visible embodiment of the Kingdom of God.

Why not live here and now as we will live when we rise with glorified bodies.

Why not go about doing good and speaking of the Kingdom of God when the opportunity presents itself.

2nd Sunday of Lent (B) 2018

Why do we say that the Mass is central to our Catholic Faith?

This is so because everything that God has ever done or said is encapsulated, summarised, condensed, in the one act or event of the crucifixion of Jesus of Nazareth.

God my Creator's last word, final testament, definitive act, most visible demonstration of His concern, care and commitment to my total welfare is the crucifixion.

As St. Paul says in Rom. 5; 'For while we were still sinners, at the right time Christ died for the ungodly. Indeed, rarely will anyone die for a righteous person though perhaps for a good person someone might actually dare to die. But God proves his love for us in that while we still were sinners Christ died for us.'

The Mass is what we do to remember, to re-enact, to re-present the crucifixion, in the way that Jesus of Nazareth asked us to do it.

At the Last Supper, taking bread he shared it among them to eat saying 'this is my body which will be given up for you.' (given up for you tomorrow on the cross). Then taking the wine he poured some for each of them to drink saying 'this is my blood which will be shed for you.' (shed for you tomorrow on the cross). Then he added `do this in memory of me.' This act (the Mass) which we do in memory of him is the simple enactment or representation of the Last Supper. The Last Supper is the symbolic reenactment or representation of what was to happen the following day on the cross.

Therefore our eyes and mind should be focused on the crucifix during mass rather than on the bread and wine. The crucifixion is what is really happening, the bread and wine are symbols re-presenting the crucifixion.

(That is why there is always a crucifix on or near the altar during Mass.)

The original Mass was a group of people sitting round the kitchen table in a private house, reading from some part of the Old Testament, singing a few psalms and sharing a loaf of bread and a flagon of wine while repeating the words of Jesus at the Last Supper. The principal emotion or motivation was gratitude and thanksgiving for the great things God had and is doing for them. Then they left, each going their own way, to live and spread the good news of the kingdom of God.

Because of large numbers, big churches and the accumulation over the years of prayers and some out of date symbols, this simple act of remembrance and gratitude is not easily discernible today. One has to work at it and concentrate closely.

Human nature being human nature, one's motivation and gratitude at any particular Mass, can vary from strong to non existent. The latter is where faith and raw commitment come into play. (One might say, just like married life).

3rd Sunday of Lent (B) 2018

All four Gospels relate the incident in the temple in Jerusalem because they saw it as having major symbolic consequences for Jews and Christians alike. The Jews saw it as a rejection of the Temple as the centre of their religion, as the dwelling place of their God, as the major unifying factor of their nation.

Even at that time Jews came in their thousands from all over the world to offer sacrifice and prayer in the temple, especially for the great feast of the Passover when this incident occurred.

It is reckoned that at that time, during Passover week, the population of Jerusalem jumped from 20 thousand to 120 thousand. It was a time of extreme political and religious tension when every available soldier and policeman was on constant duty.

By his actions and words, that day in the Temple, Jesus of Nazareth effectively and openly rejected all this cherished belief and custom.

Being immediately aware of the meaning of his words and actions the temple guards and authorities immediately descended on him demanding a spectacular sign from heaven (some jaw dropping miracle) showing that he had authority from God for doing what he had just done.

Jesus' reply was 'destroy this temple and in three days I will raise it up.'

The meaning of these words were understood by the followers of Jesus a week later when he was executed, buried and arose from the dead after three days.

From now on the Temple; the dwelling of God, is the person of Jesus of Nazareth. From now on true worship is not that offered in the old temple in Jerusalem such as burnt offerings and the sacrifice of animals, not long prayers and much singing of psalms, not clouds of incense and solemn and protracted liturgies and cultic worship. From now on the Temple is the person of Jesus of Nazareth who lives among us and in whom God lives in His fullness. From now on the temple or the church or the mosque are just convenient buildings where the children of God meet to give praise and thanks to their God. True worship is following in the footsteps of Jesus of Nazareth, walking hand in hand with Jesus of Nazareth, living in the Spirit of Jesus of Nazareth. True worship is living in constant awareness that we are all one family, God's Family. That we are all responsible for one another. That all we have is a gift from our God and must be shared with generosity. From now on there is only one commandment, one precept, one teaching - 'But to you who hear I say, love your enemies, do good to those who hate you. Bless those who curse you, pray for those who mistreat you .... then your reward will be great and you will be children of the Most High, for he himself is kind to the ungrateful and the wicked.'

I well know that I will never fully comply with this. Just as I well know that I will never win the half marathon or even the 10k fun run. But that need not stop one from running.

4th Sunday of Lent (B) 2018

"For God so loved the world that he gave his only Son, so that everyone who believes in him might not perish but might have eternal life. For God did not send his Son into the world to condemn the world, but that the world might be saved through him."

For God's own reasons (inexplicable to us) God loved the world (all creation) from the very beginning. In more scientific terms God loves all matter and whatever matter produced, developed into or evolved into, from the very beginning.

Love (God's love) was the trigger, the motivation, the catalyst for creation. Love seeks reciprocation. Inanimate, non-sentient and sentient creation reciprocate God's love by being true to their nature (e.g. a stone exists as a stone and does not try to be a plant.)

Intelligent creation (human beings) can also recognise and understand God's goodness and love and reciprocate in like manner.

From the very beginning God's motivation was, and is, the sharing of God's life, existence, being and love. This involved God's revealing Itself (demonstrating what God is like) to creation. Firstly by the work of God's hands (creation itself), secondly through the writings of Scripture (the Bible etc.) and thirdly through the Incarnation (God becoming a human being and being born, living and dying among us).

The Incarnation was not an antidote, an adjustment, a repair job necessitated by the fall of man (Original sin). The

Incarnation was part of God's plan from the very beginning (part of God's ongoing plan of self-revelation). God's plan for creation was not and never will be disrupted or put in jeopardy by anything human beings did or will do or not do.

Salvation is knowing God through God's self-revelation and responding to this knowledge in spirit and in truth. "This is the verdict, that the light came into the world, but people preferred darkness to light, because their works were evil." "But whoever lives the truth comes to the light."

God is light, God is truth, God is straightforwardness, God is genuine, God is authentic. Worshipping God is not about doing certain things or acting in a certain way. It is about being a certain sort of person.

"Jesus said to her. Woman, believe me, the hour is coming when you will worship the Father neither on this mountain nor in Jerusalem. ... But the hour is coming, and is now here, when the true worshippers will worship the Father in spirit and truth, for the Father seeks such as these to worship him. God is spirit, and those who worship him must worship in spirit and truth."

That is why Jesus said; "If any want to become my followers, let them deny themselves and take up their cross and follow me. For those who want to save their life will lose it, and those who lose their life for my sake will find it."

This is about genuinely putting others first. Genuinely being compassionate. Genuinely being forgiving. Genuinely being tolerant. Genuinely being generous. It is not just about acting in a loving way but being genuinely loving. Not just about donating to the needy but believing that what is yours is only held in stewardship for helping others etc.

This is the cross that Jesus tells his followers they must take up. The cross is self-denial. The cross is selflessness. The cross is putting the needs and the wellbeing of others before one's own. This is what 'losing ones life' for Jesus' sake means. By being genuinely generous, putting others and their needs first, being unselfish, one is taking up one's cross and following Jesus.

Religion is worshipping God in spirit and in truth.

Religions are human organisations which seek to guide me towards worshipping God in spirit and in truth. Religions are there to constantly remind me what worshipping God in spirit and in truth means. Religions are there to help me to worship God in spirit and in truth. Religions are there to help me to take up my cross every day and follow Jesus of Nazareth.

Holy Thursday (B) 2018

The message today is twofold.

What we call the Mass is the memorial of the events of today in the life of Jesus of Nazareth.

It is the memorial of the Last Supper which Jesus and his disciples cerebrated on Thursday evening just before he was arrested. During the Last Supper He told them to 'do this in memory of him.'

Every time we celebrate Mass we do again what was done at the Last Supper to remember the life, death and Resurrection of Jesus of Nazareth - God made man.

But the Church teaches us that it is not just a memorial like a photograph of or a headstone to a deceased loved one. The Mass is the re-presentation - the actual presenting again - of the life, death and Resurrection of Jesus of Nazareth, here and now, so that I and you can experience and participate in it as the followers of Jesus participated in it two thousand years ago in Palestine.

This amazing and mysterious memorial; re-presentation, to have meaning to me, to have an effect on my life and my understanding of God, must be accompanied with, must be integrated with the washing of feet. The washing of feet is actual service to our fellow human beings as well as a symbol of service. As Jesus said 'the Son of Man did not come to be served but to serve.'

FATHER JOHN

This is the hard bit for me. This is the part I like to lay aside for the time being. This is the part I like to put on the long finger. This is the part I must deliberately scrutinise, appraise, judge myself on, and practise, today and tomorrow and Saturday etc. if I want to experience the Resurrection and new life in Christ this Easter.

Good Friday (B) 2018

The events of Good Friday can evoke much sorrow, grief and guilt.

There is much reference to Christ's carrying our sins, reconciling us to the Father, paying our debt of sin, being punished for our wrongdoing etc. both in Scripture and in Church teaching.

But this is not the whole story by a long shot.

The life, suffering and death of Jesus of Nazareth was not God's response to the sinfulness of man. It was part of God's plan, even before the beginning of creation. It was part of God's plan of self-revelation to creation as creation progressively evolved.

As I have mentioned in previous occasions the catalyst for creation was God's love. Love is outgoing. Love seeks a lover. Love seeks reciprocating love. To this end God seeks to reveal Itself to the object of Its love. Inanimate and sentient creatures reciprocate God's love by being what they are. But Human beings, having evolved intelligence and self awareness, cannot only reciprocate by being and living in accordance with their created nature but can also know, appreciate and love the Creator.

We, human beings can know God in three ways;

Through the works of God's hands. Understanding, appreciating and caring for nature. Studying and understanding Scripture.

Through the life, death and resurrection of Jesus of Nazareth - God made man.

So the Incarnation (God becoming a human being) was always part of God's plan of self- revelation to his creation.

This does not mean that God willed that Jesus of Nazareth should be arrested, tortured and executed as a criminal on a cross. What it does mean is that God became a man to demonstrate to us what God was like in the most graphic way possible (by becoming a human being just like you and I). That this demonstration of what God is like, this demonstration of God's care, compassion, generosity, sharing, forgiveness, tolerance etc. was totally unacceptable to both civil and religious authorities was not God's doing but the result of human self interest, greed and lust for power.

To foresee this outcome resulting from the preaching and lifestyle of Jesus of Nazareth was not difficult. His mother and relatives saw it. (they thought he had lost his mind and came to bring him home). The Apostles saw it and tried to dissuade him from going to Jerusalem. The civil and religious authorities made no secret of their desire to get rid of him.

Obviously Jesus of Nazareth could have walked away from this inevitable outcome at any stage right up to Thursday evening in the Garden of Gethsemane. He could easily have taken to his heels and disappeared across the many national boarders in the region at that time. Who would have blamed him?

The answer is He would have blamed himself. He would have surrendered to the forces of injustice and oppression, to the forces of evil in the world.

So he stayed true to his fight for justice and peace. He stayed loyal to his lifestyle and teaching. He stayed true to those suffering injustice and oppression, to those who couldn't disappear quietly over a border to save themselves. He stayed true to the very core of his message - which is death to self interest and life in service to others.

The message today is that should you or I try to live as Jesus of Nazareth lived.

Should you or I try to truly live as Christians. We too would be such an embarrassment, such a challenge, such a threat, to civil and religious authorities that we too would be sidelined, defamed, slandered, ridiculed, subverted, laughed out of court and neutralised.

We see this happen every day to people who fight for justice, and peace.

See the fate of whistleblowers.

Just watch those, presently fighting for Gun control in the U.S.

Easter (B) 2018

Easter is the culmination, the end point, of God's plan for his creation.

We think of Resurrection as pertaining only to human beings. That is, that of all creation only we human beings will rise from death with glorified bodies as Jesus of Nazareth did.

(Remember that, with a glorified body, Mary of Magdala and his apostles and disciples who knew him intimately, did not initially recognise him after the Resurrection)

But St. Paul tells us "I consider that the sufferings of this present time are as nothing compared with the glory to be revealed for us. For creation awaits with eager expectation the revelation of the children of God; in hope that creation itself would be set free from slavery to corruption and share in the glorious freedom of the children of God. We know that all creation is groaning in labor pains even until now; and not only that, but we ourselves, who have the first fruits of the Spirit, we also groan within ourselves as we wait for adoption, the redemption of our bodies."

In other words, it is not only we human beings who await resurrection and glorification but also the whole of creation (all that exists or ever existed).

Our bodies, as they are, are prone to corruption (death and decomposition).

Not only our bodies but also all created matter. We, our bodies and all of creation are (as St. Paul says) groaning in labour, waiting for salvation, redemption, resurrection, the glorious freedom of the children of God, call it what you like.

This is the final self-revelation of the Creator to us human beings and to all creation.

So the risen and glorified Jesus of Nazareth is our future, our destiny, our hope, our fulfillment. The risen and glorified Jesus of Nazareth is gathering all of creation to himself so that all things in heaven and on earth may be one again with the Creator from whom all creation began its great journey and adventure of existence, of being and life.

So let us rejoice and be glad. Alleluia, alleluia, alleluia.

2nd Sunday of Easter (B) 2018

Christ has died.
Christ is risen.
We are people of the Resurrection.

Resurrection infuses our total outlook, our total existence, our whole attitude, to things, to people, to ourselves, to our God.

Our every experience, everything that happens to us, our every thought and desire, floats on, is buoyed up by, our total belief in and joyful acceptance of Resurrection from death and Eternal Life in and with our Creator.

John 6: "I have come down from heaven, not to do my own will, but the will of him who sent me. And this is the will of him who sent me, that I should lose nothing of all that he has given me, but raise it up on the last day. This is indeed the will of my Father, that all who see the Son and believe in him may have eternal life; and I will raise them up on the last day." Without belief in Resurrection each of our lives consists of just so many rolls of the dice. Each roll brings its gain or its loss. But the last one is always the one where we lose everything.

It is firm belief in Resurrection from death and Eternal life with our Creator that brings to our lives fulfillment of the words of Scripture; "Every valley shall be filled and every mountain and hill shall be made low. The winding roads shall be made straight, and the rough ways made smooth."

It is this faith that brings equanimity to my life. That enables me to receive the joys with gratitude and accept the sorrows and pains with understanding and patient endurance. We sit for a while as we let our gratitude to our God for the gift of Resurrection, flow freely from our heart and spirit.

3rd Sunday of Easter (B) 2018

'Then he opened their minds to understand the scriptures.

And he said to them : "Thus it is written that the Messiah would suffer and rise from the dead on the third day and that repentance, for the forgiveness of sins, would be preached in his name to all the nations, beginning from Jerusalem. You are witnesses of these things."

Our capacity for self - deception is bottomless.

I can assiduously comply with all the external demands of religion; attend church, contribute money, receive Sacraments, pray, help those in need from time to time, give of my time and energy etc. and at the same time avoid forgiving actual or perceived hurts.

I can happily cherish vengeful inclinations in my heart and expect forgiveness for my own trespasses.

I can run to my God for mercy and forgiveness while planning the downfall of my perceived enemies.

My God must be very tolerant, have a very highly developed sense of humour, when He doesn't respond to my oft repeated prayer "forgive us our trespasses as we forgive those who trespass against us," with a nearby lightening strike !!!

Let us sit for a few minutes and ponder what "repentance, for the forgiveness of sins" means.

4th Sunday of Easter (B) 2018

There are two sorts of prayer. One is a private conversation, or communion or communication between you and your God. It is private, personal and intimate.

The second is an official, community or family function with a set form and intent.

The Mass is this second form of prayer.

A couple of things today which might improve, enliven, enhance, our Masses for ourselves and for God our Father.

What is all important is the attitude we have, our approach to, our understanding of, what our Mass is about.

Mass is a family, a community gathering, a get together, a celebration of, our bond as one family - Gods family.

We come together as one united family - God's family here in our church. We come together in response to our Father's invitation to his children to join Him at table and to rejoice in our unity as one family. We, brothers and sisters, God's beloved children, gather together in mutual respect and love, to rejoice together and with God, as God's family, and express, as one family, our gratitude and respect to God our Father.

Imagine grandparents throwing a party on the occasion of their golden wedding anniversary. They invite all their children, grandchildren, great grandchildren as well as some long standing relatives and friends. Imagine the greetings, laughter, handshakes, hugs, chatter etc. as they meet, exchange news, coo over the latest crop of babies and generally catch up with family news and events. Of course each one greets the grandparents first but then mix freely with all others.

Of course at the proper time, all are called to order and to give their undivided attention to the official programme, speeches, and presentation of gifts.

That is my understanding of the celebration of Mass. That is why I encourage you to get to know each other especially those sitting near to you. That is why I encourage you to sit in different locations from time to time. That is why I try to greet you as you enter rather than as you leave. That is why we have hospitality in the hall after 9.30 mass on Sundays. That is why I am happy to see you getting to know each other and chatting together before Mass. It goes without saying that all the clergy do not share this understanding and attitude.

Of course the time comes when all the above ceases and we give our undivided attention to the official celebration.

How I join in the responses of the Mass is a very good indication of the degree of my understanding of, and participation in, this family celebration. Synchronised responses with a pleasing volume will help me to appreciate my part in this community celebration in honour of God our Father and in gratitude for God's many gifts.

I always maintain that if I participate well in the Mass; If I participate mentally, emotionally and verbally, then I will, and should, feel tired at the end of Mass but also content and happy.

A Mass where the responses are given in unity of voice, with enthusiastic volume, is a joy to the ear and uplifting to the mind and soul for all present.

This does not just happen; it must be worked on and brought about.

5th Sunday of Easter (B) 2018

I remember well when I was seven or eight years old, having heard somewhere that one should not damage the bark of a tree, especially that one should not cut the bark of a tree all around; this was called ringing a tree. Curious to see what would happen, I ringed a nice ash tree which was about a foot in diameter. This tree did not belong to us. Some time later my father noticed it. I haven't ringed any trees ever since.

For some time the tree showed no signs of damage in the branches and leaves but gradually the foliage began to wilt and die. By the following spring the tree was well and truly dead and was cut down and burned as firewood. I have always regretted this act of vandalism for a number of reasons.

Today's Gospel uses this as a simile of what happens when I lose contact with Jesus of Nazareth. I am cut off from the sap of the Spirit. I begin to wilt. I begin to drift away from the church community. I begin to not pray. I begin to attend the Mass less frequently and then not at all. I seldom think of God and then only when disaster strikes.

Spiritually I die and can only be used as 'firewood.' From time to time some of you have asked me about someone who was once part of our parish community. Have they moved house you ask? Are they unwell you ask? Have they died you ask? The answer of course is yes - they have been ringed and died spiritually.

This is nothing strange. A once strong friendship will, through neglect, slowly wither and die. A once single figure golf handicap will, for lack of practice, become a double figure handicap.

FATHER JOHN

A once familiarity with my God will, through neglect, become a mere nodding acquaintance.

We all know how to fix this situation - the very same way you fix your golf handicap or your neglected friendship.

6th Sunday of Easter (B) 2018

'I have told you this so that my joy may be in you and your joy may be complete.'

Jesus of Nazareth was sent to us by God, our Father and Creator, so that the love and joy which resides within the Holy Trinity - the Father, the Son and the Holy Spirit - be shared with you and I, and reside in us always.

This is what true religion means.

So any religion or religious teaching that deliberately fosters or promotes fear or unhappiness is false religion.

So also any interpretation of the Bible which promotes fear of God (that is fear as in fear of violence, fear of deliberate punishment, fear of imposed pain etc.) is a wrong interpretation of the Bible and needs to be restudied and reinterpreted.

As an aside it is important to note that our understanding of the Bible is an ongoing process. Scripture scholars are continually having new or fuller insights into our present understanding of the Scriptures. This will, and should continue to, be welcomed by us and not treated with automatic suspicion or rejection.

It is important to note that many of us, consciously or unconsciously, harbour a residual fear of our God and an inherited doubt regarding the totality of God's goodness, mercy and love for us.

It is good for me to recognise this condition in which I find myself and continually ask my God to free me from it, as it is a subtle ploy of the 'Evil One.'

This joy about which we read in today's gospel reading, which comes from God and is a gift of God, is not dependent on the earthly condition in which I find myself at any particular time. It must go much deeper than everyday events be they joys or sufferings. It must be based on the total trustworthiness, veracity, mercy and love of my God and a looking forward in great hope to resurrection from death and a sharing in the Eternal life of my God. This is something that the first followers of Jesus of Nazareth understood well.

We are told of the apostles; 'So they left the presence of the Sanhedrin, rejoicing that they had been found worthy to suffer dishonour for the sake of the name."

And again of St Paul; 'This man is a chosen instrument of mine to carry my name before Gentiles, kings, and Israelites, and I will show him what he will have to suffer for my name." There are no promises of a comfortable ride here.

Pentecost Sunday (B) 2018

"Jesus said to them again, Peace be with you. As the Father has sent me, so I send you. And when he had said this, he breathed on them and said to them, Receive the Holy Spirit. Whose sins you forgive are forgiven them, and whose sins you retain are retained."

The Council of Trent (1545 - 1563) defined that this power to forgive sins is exercised in the Sacrament of Penance (or as we call it today; the Sacrament of Reconciliation).

This does not say, or mean, that the Sacrament of Reconciliation is the only way the Church (the Christian Community) exercises the power to forgive sins.

For instance the Christian Community exercises the power to forgive sins in the Sacrament of Baptism.

The Christian Community exercises the power to forgive sins in the Sacrament of The Anointing of the Sick.

The sinner oneself, who is genuinely sorry for and regrets any harm, hurt or damage caused and sincerely tries to repair any such harm, damage or hurt, receives forgiveness of sin. There is no compelling reason to believe that when the events described in today's Gospel reading took place there were only the ten Apostles present (The next verse tells us that the Apostle Thomas was not present). The people in the room are described as the Disciples. This would include a very mixed group of Jesus' followers including Apostles and disciples, both men and women.

It is this group or gathering or family of Jesus' followers who were given His (Jesus') power to forgive sin.

Naturally in an endemically patriarchal culture as existed at that time (and is still to be found today) an important ability such as that to forgive sin (as well as leadership roles generally within the Christian Community) would be cornered by the male gender and particularly by those in leadership positions.

(The latter is just common sense, and how things generally pan out in all aspects of human society.)

Having said all the above I now want to look at the essential role played by both the sinner and the victim in the process of repentance, reconciliation and forgiveness. It is very difficult, if not impossible, for the sinner to obtain healing and repentance if the victim refuses to forgive. This refusal only increases the hurt and bitterness in both parties. But if the victim welcomes any movement towards reconciliation on the part of the sinner then the flood-gates of healing and reconciliation begin to open for both parties. The above examples illustrate the words of today's Gospel reading 'Whose sins you forgive are forgiven them, and whose sins you retain are retained."

Events occurring during the truth and reconciliation commission in South Africa graphically demonstrated those words of Jesus.

To my way of thinking this way of forgiveness, of reconciliation, of healing, fits in nicely with the example and actions of Jesus of Nazareth, rather than the more mechanical and impersonal 'secret confession to a priest' who has no involvement in the whole affair.

Therefore I, as a Christian, must face up to my ability and responsibility to facilitate forgiveness for those who sin against me, in any way, by my attitude and willingness to go at least half way.

The attitude of the father of the prodigal son must be my guiding star.

Trinity Sunday (B) 2018

The first Commandment of God to the whole of creation is; 'I, the LORD, am your God. You shall not have other gods besides me.'

This is the central and main doctrine of the Bible.

To this day the heart of, and the reason for, all Jewish worship is the cry; 'Hear, 0 Israel! The LORD is our God, the LORD alone.'

This great commandment, this great cry of allegiance, is also the heart of Christianity and the centre of all our worship.

The existence of the Holy Trinity was unknown in the Old Testament. (Although there were hints or references pointing towards it.)

One of the most important revelations brought to us by Jesus of Nazareth was the existence of three distinct Persons in the One God (the Holy Trinity). Firstly, we learned something of the relationship that exists between the Three Persons. Secondly, what you might describe as the sphere of influence or speciality of each Person and thirdly, what their individual relationship with creation might be.

You might say that this pushes back slightly the cloak of mystery surrounding God the Creator.

This revelation concerning the Holy Trinity enables us to draw certain tentative conclusions. Our God is a community or family.

The relationship within this family is one of total unity and love.

This love, of its very nature, seeks to share itself with other things. Hence creation.

The proper response of creation to this sharing must be as part of this unified community. It always puzzled me as to why God bothered to create.

For me the answer was to be found in the relationship within the Holy Trinity Family. The internal love existing within the Holy Trinity family was such as to compel that family to share that love. True love reaches out, seeks to share that love. To reach out in love to others God had to create those others first.

St John tells us; 'We have come to know and to believe in the love God has for us. God is love, and whoever remains in love remains in God and God in them.' And again; 'For God so loved the world that he gave his only Son.'

We are attracted to a family where mutual respect and love exists.

One seeks a loving couple when looking for adoptive parents.

The reason is that love tends to reach out, to share, to encompass others.

We were created because of love. We are encompassed by love. We return to the love that created us.

Religion is realising this and responding to it.

Corpus Christi (B) 2108

Most of us have a photograph, or piece of music, or some household article, or piece of jewellery, or some saying or story etc. which we associate with a parent or parents. We treasure this because of its associations with someone we love, because of the memories it brings back.

For the same reason we see people putting some object on a coffin or on a grave. These are symbols of the love that person has for us and we have for them.

'God so loved the world that he gave his only Son.'

'In this way the love of God was revealed to us: God sent his only Son into the world so that we might have life through him.'

Jesus of Nazareth is the living symbol of the love God the Creator has for me. 'Do this in memory of me' Jesus said at the Last Supper.

'For as often as you eat this bread and drink the cup, you proclaim the death of the Lord until he comes.' said St. Paul.

That is why we are gathered here today.

That is why we look on the image of Jesus of Nazareth executed on a cross.

That is why we bow down in reverence before what seems to be simple bread and wine.

The Eucharist. Holy Communion. The Body and Blood of Jesus of Nazareth. The Breaking of Bread. The Mass. Call it what you like. It is the great symbol of Immanuel. Of 'God with me.'

Jesus says; 'I pray not only for them, but also for those who will believe in me through their word, so that they may all be one, as you, Father, are in me and I in you, that they also may be in us, that the world may believe that you sent me. And I have given them the glory you gave me, so that they may be one, as we are one, I in them and you in me, that they may be brought to perfection as one.'

I do not need to go anywhere to be one with my God. The Eucharist is the symbol and the guarantee of this. Life is walking in the presence of my God at all times, in all places, in all circumstances. We come together in one place as one family to confirm our oneness with our God and to thank God, as one united family, for this great gift.

We need to come together as one family (God's Family) every week, expressing our gratitude for 'Immanuel', otherwise all the above becomes vague and woolly and ceases to exercise any influence on my life and conduct.

10th Sunday of the Year (B) 2018

Jesus of Nazareth's preaching and lifestyle was a great scandal, a great embarrassment, a great challenge, not only to the religious and political authorities but also to his family and relatives, including his mother. For the authorities it challenged their power and privilege. To his family it meant scrutiny from the authorities and the near certainty that their Jesus would be arrested and maybe executed. So his family made a number of attempts to dissuade him and bring him back home, by force if necessary. (What mother wants to lose her only child !!). So forget about any presumption you had that his family and relatives were all behind him and supportive.

Belief in Jesus of Nazareth only came to his family after the resurrection. We also seldom realise that the same was true for many of the priests, Scribes and Pharisees. Certainly nothing like the majority but a substantial number became Christians. As we read in Acts. at the council of Jerusalem. "some from the party of the Pharisees who had become believers stood up and said, It is necessary to circumcise them and direct them to observe the Mosaic law." (In other words they wanted Gentiles to officially become Jews before becoming Christians). Belief in the Resurrection of Jesus of Nazareth from the dead was the decisive factor which prompted the Apostles and so many early Christians to give their lives for the faith. It was the decisive factor which finally changed the minds of his family and relatives. It was the decisive factor which prompted many of his one time enemies to become Christian. It was the decisive factor in the conversion of St. Paul.

Are you convinced of the Resurrection?

Are we perhaps just covering both wickets?

Does belief in Resurrection enliven your day, make your grief bearable, lift your joys to a new level, give meaning to the hum-drum of life, inspire you to volunteer your time and abilities in helping others, make the aches and pains of old age acceptable?

If not then get with Resurrection from death and Eternal life with and in your God.

11th Sunday of the Year (B) 2018

Jesus of Nazareth was sent by the Holy Trinity to tell us about, and to inaugurate, the Kingdom of Heaven or the Kingdom of God.

This Kingdom of God is everything that the kingdoms of this world are not.

Take any aspect of government, of royalty, of dictatorship and you will find that the Kingdom of God is the direct opposite.

We find this unnerving. We find it very hard to swallow. We find it very difficult to accept and practise.

'Blessed are the poor in spirit. Blessed are the meek. "It is like a mustard seed which is the smallest seed you plant in the ground.' Whoever humbles himself like this child is the greatest in the kingdom of heaven. "it will be hard for one who is rich to enter the kingdom of heaven."It is like yeast that a woman took and mixed (in) with three measures of wheat flour until the whole batch of dough was leavened."When you give alms, do not let your left hand know what your right is doing.'

Moses was on the run from the Egyptian police when God called him to lead the Israelites to freedom. He had a bad stutter and had to have Aaron to speak for him.

David was not even considered by his father when Samuel came to anoint one of his sons king. They had to send someone to call him from where he was herding the sheep and goats in the bush. Jesus of Nazareth himself came from one of the poorest hamlets in the poverty stricken province of Galilee.

'Can anything good come from Nazareth?' was Nathaniel's reply when told that Jesus was from Nazareth. Jesus called his twelve Apostles not from the religious leaders or the privileged classes but from everyday working people.

Lastly, our exemplar, our Leader, our God is executed on a cross as a subversive and a criminal.

I could profitably spend some time thinking about the following quotation from Jesus of Nazareth - the convicted and executed criminal - who is my God.

This I command you: love one another. If the world hates you, realise that it hated me first. If you belonged to the world, the world would love its own; but because you do not belong to the world, and I have chosen you out of the world, the world hates you.'

So do I belong to the 'world' or to the Criminal?

BIRTH OF JOHN THE BAPTIST (B)
2018

'Amen, I say to you, among those born of women there has been none greater than John the Baptist.'

Why did Jesus of Nazareth describe John the Baptist in those words?

For Jesus of Nazareth, John was greater that Abraham, than Isaac, than Jacob, than Samuel, Elijah, David, and Solomon. For him John was greater than Peter or Paul or any of the Apostles. For him John was greater than his mother, than Mary of Magdala or anyone else you can think of.

I wonder why?

For me the reason is that at the height of his physical and mental abilities (he was only 30), at the height of his popularity and power (he was so popular and had such a large dedicated following that neither political leaders nor religious leaders could touch him despite his excoriating them for their hypocrisy and immorality) he urged and even ordered his followers to follow and listen to this newcomer called Jesus of Nazareth.

He was well aware of what this would mean for him, and what very soon happened. With the departure of most of his followers to join Jesus of Nazareth his political and religious enemies had him quickly arrested, jailed and executed without trial.

John the Baptist was the greatest because he had no personal desire for greatness; it was thrust upon him by God.

He accepted greatness and immediately abandoned greatness as his God willed, although the latter came at a terrible price.

He underwent much soul-searching and was plagued by doubts as we read in the Gospels: From prison "John summoned two of his disciples and sent them to the Lord to ask – "Are you the one who is to come, or should we look for another?"

It is amazing that we have all sorts of people within our church urging us to pray to this saint or that saint, to practise this devotion or that devotion but I have never heard of anyone urging us to pray to John the Baptist or pushing a devotion to John the Baptist!!!

This is John the Baptist. This is what he was and is like. He steps aside. He relinquishes power gladly. He does not promote himself. He likes the background. For him it is only God who matters. It is God he promotes. He eschews showy devotions. He is not the patron saint of anything. He was never canonised (as far as I know). You do not see statues of him in churches surrounded by votive lights and vases of flowers. Have you ever seen a prayer to John the Baptist?

And yet according to Jesus of Nazareth - God the Son the Second person of the Blessed Trinity - he is the greatest.

For me his greatness is in his humility and his total dedication to the will of his God.

13th Sunday of the Year (B) 2018

There was a woman afflicted with haemorrhages for twelve years.'

Central to this event is Leviticus 15. 'When a woman is afflicted with a flow of blood .... she shall be unclean, just as during her menstrual period.'

As you can imagine a patriarchal Old Testament was not female friendly.

In the Old Testament being unclean meant that (like lepers) you could have no contact with God or other human beings. You were forbidden the synagogue and its prayers and devotions. Anything or anyone you touched became unclean.

So this woman was not only physically sick but also regarded as spiritually sick and ostracised by everyone. She could not even have the consolation of recourse to her religion and her God.

All this through no fault of her own. She was the victim but punished as the perpetrator. Imagine her relief and joy not only at her physical cure but at the words of Jesus; 'Daughter, our Tamil has made you well; go in peace, and be healed of your affliction.'

How many Catholics are experiencing the same exclusion and sense of guilt as this unfortunate woman? How many Catholics feel excluded from their church and their God because of some clergy who think and act like the Pharisees. Pope Francis is trying to apply the mind of Christ to all these moral teachings and practises but is meeting unyielding opposition.

The church is given authority to lead people to God by its teaching and practises. Nobody has the authority to act as a stumbling block for others in their search for God.

Pope Francis is trying to teach us to take responsibility for our own decisions in religious and moral matters. This particularly in marital and sexual problems.

There are plenty of embezzlers, thieves, liars, corrupt officials, drug dealers, human traffickers etc. walking around freely and nobody is telling them that they cannot receive Holy Communion.

But have some marital or sexual problem and the whole weight of ecclesiastical law lands on your head!!!

If you are excluding yourself or have been told to exclude yourself from Holy Communion, think long and hard about how you are treating your God - not as a loving and compassionate parent but as an unforgiving and small-minded overseer.

14th Sunday of the Year (B) 2018

One of the hardest things to do is to change when we already believe that we know it all. I call it the 'we always did it this way' syndrome or 'that is what we were always told' syndrome.

I know all about this syndrome as I suffered from it for many, many years and still do to some extent.

Actually many of us clergy suffer from this syndrome.

The simple people of Nazareth suffered from this syndrome. They knew all there was to know about their neighbour, Jesus of Nazareth. They remembered when he was born, they knew his mother and father (had they not been at his father's funeral?). They knew his cousins and relatives. They could point out unerringly his goats and sheep from all the other livestock of the village.

They had heard the stories about his doings elsewhere, about his preaching, even that miracles and cures were attributed to him.

They could not get their heads around all this. There was some mistake, there was some trickery involved. Was this not the boy and man they had known for thirty years? What was all the brouhaha about?

When Jesus arrived in Nazareth with his disciples no crowds were there to meet him. There were no sick clamouring for cures. It was only in the Synagogue, at the usual Sabbath prayers, that he met all the people of Nazareth.

All the stuff they had heard just couldn't be true (after all was this not the carpenter, Mary's son, who had disappeared suddenly some time back?) and of course the inevitable mix of envy and jealousy at the possibility that there was some truth in what they had been hearing.

How could they possibly admit that they had got it wrong!

In the same way today it is some of the people of our own church who refuse to accept and listen to Pope Francis. It is some in the leadership of our own Church who are the most vociferous of his opponents.

To quote today's Gospel; 'Where did this man get all this. They said......And they took offence at him.'

Our present Pope is trying to revive the hope and joy engendered during Vatican II. He is giving us an example to follow. One of mercy, tolerance, acceptance, forgiveness and love. He is asking each one of us to change, to be converted, to be renewed.

I must be willing to listen and to change. This is the part I don't like.

15TH SUNDAY OF THE YEAR (B) 2018

Today's Gospel reading has a few interesting points.

1) Jesus gives his Apostles authority over evil spirits. Evil spirits are whatever prevents or obstructs me from following the example of Jesus of Nazareth; obstructs me from walking in the presence of God; from being guided by the Holy Spirit. In other words Jesus of Nazareth gives his followers - his church - the authority to bring healing and freedom from whatever prevents me from following Jesus of Nazareth. These evil spirits are pride, covetousness, lust, anger, gluttony, envy and sloth.

This authority has nothing to do with "you do it this way' or 'you do it our way' or else ...

It is authority or power to bring healing and freedom to those who need and want it. It has nothing to do with control or coercion.

2) The Gospel reading goes on to mention a number of details as regards how to dress or not dress, what to carry or not carry with them. How to act in differing circumstances. These may have been relevant 2000 years ago but today they must be taken as symbolic; indicating the right attitude and approach to their mission.

Their influence must have nothing to do with showy fanfare, displays of wealth or political clout.

Their influence must come from service to others, from bringing healing, peace of heart and freedom of spirit.

They must come bringing gifts; the gift of the Good News of the Kingdom of God. The gift of Salvation.

Listen to the following from St. Luke:

Jesus came to Jericho and intended to pass through the town. Now a man there named Zacchaeus, who was a chief tax collector and also a wealthy man, was seeking to see who Jesus was; but he could not see him because of the crowd, for he was short in stature. So he ran ahead and climbed a sycamore tree in order to see Jesus, who was about to pass that way.

When he reached the place, Jesus looked up and said to him, Zacchaeus, come down quickly, for today I must stay at your house. And he came down quickly and received him with joy. When they all saw this, they began to grumble, saying, He has gone to stay at the house of a sinner. But Zacchaeus stood there and said to the Lord, Behold, half of my possessions,

Lord, I shall give to the poor, and if I have extorted anything from anyone I shall repay it four times over. And Jesus said to him. Today salvation has come to this house.'

This clearly demonstrates the authority and power given by Jesus of Nazareth to his church; to his followers - the power to bring spiritual healing, to bring spiritual freedom, spiritual peace and salvation. Nothing more. Nothing less.

17th Sunday of the Year (B) 2018

To get away for a while, Jesus and his Apostles crossed over to the far shore of the Sea of Galilee in a boat. Watching them go, those with a boat available crossed over following them. Many more walked all around the lake to join up with them on the far shore. Seeing this great crowd coming towards him and gathering around him Jesus knew that they were very tired and hungry.

His first concern was their physical needs. He asked Philip if they could buy bread for them. Philip replied that they had no money for this but the little food they had - 5 barley loves and two fish - they could share.

Whenever I begin to feel sorry for myself I remind myself of the 34,361 migrants and refugees known to have died while fleeing oppression, war and poverty in their own countries and attempting to find a new home within the borders of the EU. These are only those known to have died: the actual figure is much higher. The names of over 90% of the former are unknown. Their families will never know what happened to them or where they were buried, if they were buried.

Whenever I begin to think that I am seriously trying to be a Christian. Whenever I begin to think that I am doing my bit as a Christian, I have to remind myself of my complacency concerning the thousands of bodies washed up on our shores.

Jesus of Nazareth is asking me 'where shall we buy bread for these people to eat?" Where shall we find a place for these people to live?" "Where shall we find work for these people to do?"

The above is a very good reality check for me. It brings me down to earth. It shows me clearly how far I am prepared to go 'to love my neighbour as myself.' Not very far at all.

As St. Paul said concerning the tendency to think that he was doing well, to think that he was a good Christian: "Therefore, to keep me from being too elated, a thorn was given me in the flesh, ... to keep me from being too elated."

Today, the plight of migrants and refugees is 'the thorn in the flesh' that shows me how far I fall short of being a real Christian.

The greatest block to God's helping me is my pride.

Pride is thinking that I can 'pray God' into doing something for me or for others. If it does come about I immediately credit myself with it.

Pride is feeling pleased with myself for donating to some worthy cause when from God's point of view I am only sharing with others what is rightfully theirs.

I need to constantly remind myself of how far I fall short. My attitude to migrants and refugees is a good way of doing this.

18th Sunday of the Year (B) 2018

'Then they said to him, What must we do to perform the works of God?"

Mk. 10. "As he was setting out on a journey, a man ran up, knelt down before him, and asked him, Good teacher, what must I do to inherit eternal life"

Lk. 10. "Just then a lawyer stood up to test Jesus. Teacher, he said, what must I do to inherit eternal life?"

Lk 18. "An official asked him this question, Good teacher, what must I do to inherit eternal life?"

A man asked Paul and Silas, "Sirs, what must I do to be saved?"

Mtt. 19. "Now someone approached him and said, Teacher, what good must I do to gain eternal life?"

Notice, all have asked to do something that will guarantee them Eternal Life.

In the Old Testament the Jewish religion was all about obeying the Law (religious laws and regulations). Up to quite recently our Church was largely about obeying the Law: be baptised as an infant, receive first Holy Communion, go to Confession, receive Confirmation, get married in church, be Anointed before you died, be buried in the Catholic section of the graveyard, attend Mass every Sunday, perform your Easter duties, support the church financially etc.

This attitude enables me to be a 'good' Jew or a 'good' Christian while in other respects I can be a pain.

As Jesus said; Woe to you, Scribes and Pharisees, you hypocrites. You pay tithes of mint and dill and cumin, and have neglected the weightier things of the law: justice and mercy and fidelity. But these you should have done, without neglecting the others. Blind guides, who strain out the gnat and swallow the camel! Woe to you, scribes and Pharisees, you hypocrites. You cleanse the outside of cup and dish, but inside they are full of plunder and self-indulgence. Blind Pharisee, cleanse first the inside of the cup, so that the outside also may be clean.'

What is the problem here?

Let's take an example. I can have a totally clean record as far as the police, government and church are concerned. I have never broken any law or regulation. And yet I can be an abusive marriage partner, an uncaring parent, a very difficult employer or employee, a mean and unhelpful neighbour etc. Jesus of Nazareth is upbraiding the Scribes and Pharisees because although they were totally law abiding they were without generosity, forgiveness, compassion, tolerance, and love.

I must take these words to heart because they may be applicable to me also, at least some of the time.

The Old Testament was about doing certain things which hopefully would persuade God to give me Eternal Life.

The New Testament is about living in a certain way in response to - in gratitude for - having been already offered and accepting the gift of Eternal Life.

Is my religion Old Testament or New Testament?

19TH SUNDAY OF THE YEAR (B) 2018

Today's Gospel reading from John begins at verse 41.

But if we go back to verse 40 we read ; This is indeed the will of my Father, that all who see the Son and believe in him may have eternal life; and I will raise them up on the last day.'

This statement of Jesus is very direct and very clear. I, and all of you who believe in Jesus of Nazareth will be raised up into Eternal Life on the last day, be that the day of our death or at some later date.

By Eternal Life is meant here not life as we know it going on for ever and ever (how boring that would be) but a sharing in the very life and existence of the Holy Trinity. What this is like is totally beyond our ken just as our life on earth is totally beyond the ken of a child in the womb.

Then we read; The Jews murmured about him because he said, I am the bread that came down from heaven.'

Was Jesus not the son of Joseph from Nazareth? How could he say I am the bread that came down from heaven?

But he reiterated. 'I am the living bread that came down from heaven; whoever eats this bread will live forever; and the bread that I will give is my flesh for the life of the world.' The Eucharist, which we are gathered here now to celebrate, is what Jesus was talking about.

The Eucharist; the bread that came down from heaven, is our guarantee of, our title deed to, Resurrection from death and sharing in the Eternal life of God.

Surely this Good News is worthy of rejoicing. Surely it demands an outpouring of gratitude from us.

Let us sit for a few moments and contemplate this great gift.

20th Sunday of the Year (B) 2018

Whoever eats my flesh and drinks my blood remains in me and I in them.'

Today's Gospel reading is obviously about the Eucharist.

One can easily just think about receiving the Body and Blood of Christ in the Eucharist, on this occasion, and miss the broader, the fuller meaning of Jesus' words.

Jesus goes on to say; just as the living Father sent me and I have life because of the Father, so also the one who feeds on me will have life because of me.'

I can receive the Eucharist on numerous occasions and still not be a good person.

So here Jesus is not just promoting reception of the Eucharist but promoting a way of life - a life in union with Jesus of Nazareth whose life is lived in union with God the Father.

So today's reading must be understood in the context of all the teaching of Jesus of Nazareth. As for example; Whoever loves me will keep my word, and my Father will love him, and we will come to him and make our dwelling with him.'

The message of Christianity is 'Immanuel' - God with me.

Everything to do with religion must point towards, promote, bring about, accomplish, life in union with our God and Creator.

This is the message of the Bible. This is the message of every authentic religion.

How good I am at cherry picking for my own selfish ends, to promote my own political ambitions, to secure more control!

In the verses following today's Gospel reading we read; 'Since Jesus knew that his disciples were murmuring about this, he said to them, Does this shock you? .... It is the spirit that gives life, while the flesh is of no avail. The words I have spoken to you are spirit and life.'

So everything concerning the teaching of Jesus of Nazareth must be understood in the context of spirit and life - the Spirit and the Life of God.

So religion is not just about doing but about being.

Doing stuff in religion is important; just as a means of transport is important so as to get to where you want to go. You utilise it to achieve an end.

The end is Immanuel. Living every day in the presence of and in union with God my Creator.

21ST SUNDAY OF THE YEAR (B) 2018

Today's second reading must be understood in the context and for the time in which it was written. With the latter in mind it is quite revolutionary.

This context and time was totally patriarchal. Women were the property of their fathers or husbands.

For Paul to say 'Husbands, love your wives, even as Christ loved the church and handed himself over for her.' is unbelievable for the time and context.

For Paul to say 'So husbands should love their wives as their own bodies. He who loves his wife loves himself.' is unbelievable for the time and context.

Even today in our 'advanced' western society it is often something more hoped for than achieved.

Today's first reading and Gospel reading are about faith in and commitment to the One True God.

If asked why I have faith in and why I am committed to the One True God I would find it difficult to explain. I would flounder and say this and that and at the end feel that it was somehow inadequate. If I asked you why you married your marriage partner could you give a clear, and succinct answer?

When referring to the followers; 'many of whom 'returned to their former way of life and no longer accompanied him' Jesus said 'it is the spirit that gives life, while the flesh is of no avail. The words I have spoken to you are spirit and life.'

In other words hard concrete proofs, explanations in words, are unavailable and inadequate when it comes to faith in, trust in and commitment to God. i.e. 'the flesh is of no avail.' So also proofs, explanations, words, are totally inadequate to explain why you love, trust and are committed to your marriage partner.

Then Jesus puts it in another way which only deepens the mystery; 'For this reason I have told you that no one can come to me unless it is granted him by my Father.'

So, as 'they' say; 'put that in your pipe and smoke it.'

22ND SUNDAY OF THE YEAR (B) 2018

"This people honours me with their lips, but their hearts are far from me;..........You abandon the commandment of God and hold to human tradition."

'What goes round comes round', 'History repeats itself.'

These sayings are so true. Any human organisation you like to pick, be it civic or religious, keeps repeating its mistakes over and over again down the ages. I myself and you, do we not do likewise?

Without going into the multitudinous examples to be found in human history, suffice it to say that our church is presently in the throes of the latest struggle between human tradition and the law of God. I and many of you were brought up in a church whose teaching was (to quote Jesus of Nazareth) 'rules taught by men.'

Now, on the one hand we have Pope Francis urging us, by word and example, to live by the Law of God - the law of love. of mercy. of compassion, of forgiveness, tolerance and justice. On the other hand we have those (among whom are numbered many in important church leadership positions) who fight tooth and nail to preserve and propagate "the traditions of the elders:

The latest spat was the one over Pope Francis' instruction that capital punishment can never be justified and those who claimed that this was contrary to church tradition are therefore heretical.

You and I can sometimes find this dispute confusing. While being strongly attracted by Pope Francis' approach and seeing its merits we can find that the bonds of the past still tie us down.

I like to describe the present confusion of competing approaches as the battle between service of God in fear and trembling and service of God in love and gratitude.

We. the clergy of Ireland and the UK, both priests and bishops as well as some of the laity (with of course some exceptions) are on the side of the 'elders' or else just sitting on the fence to see how things go.

Changing ones outlook and attitude is always painful and takes time and a lot of help from the Holy Spirit.

I think we need to be openly proactive and creative, for growth requires change and movement.

I look on the above disputation as healthy and good for our church. An apparent unanimity resulting from forceful compliance is unhealthy.

27TH SUNDAY OF THE YEAR (B) 2018

Today's Gospel reading is not about adultery but about misogyny and the abusive nature of marriage, for women, at that time.

Observing how Jesus of Nazareth treated the women among his followers as equals, the Pharisees tried to trap him with their question.

Firstly Jesus states God's plan for marital relations by quoting the Book of Genesis; From the beginning of creation, God made them male and female. For this reason a man shall leave his father and mother (and be joined to his wife), and the two shall become one flesh. So they are no longer two but one flesh. Therefore what God has joined together, no human being must separate.'

This is the ideal. This is what is to be aimed for, desired and fostered in marital relations. But the ideal is not always achieved. Things go wrong for any number of reasons.

So in the Old Testament and at the time of Jesus of Nazareth, when things went wrong in marriage a solution had to be found. The Jewish solution was as follows (keep in mind here that it was a very patriarchal society where women were the property of husbands or fathers and were treated as such.): All a husband had to do, and I quote from Deuteronomy; 'When a man, after marrying a woman .... is later displeased with her because he finds in her something objectionable ... he writes out a bill of divorce and hands it to her, thus dismissing her from his house.' Of course this was totally one-sided as a woman could not divorce her husband. She could not do the same.

Adultery was punishable by stoning to death. But a man was not regarded as committing adultery against his marriage or his wife if he went with another woman as his wife was his property. His fault was in diminishing the value of another man's property (his wife or daughter). If a woman did the same she was condemned to death because she had violated her marriage. In short the wife was not regarded as a partner but as part of her husband's property.

What Jesus is trying to get across here to his listeners is that this one sided treatment of women is wrong and unjust. What is true for the wife is equally true for the husband. Husbands cannot hide behind a human law or tradition which is blatantly patriarchal and self-serving to give themselves an unjust and unlawful loophole.

This astonished the Jews, not least his disciples, and I quote: Shortly after 'In the house, the disciples again questioned him about this.' They are shocked at Jesus saying that the duties and rights of husband and wife were equal; that adultery, whether by husband or wife, was equally reprehensible.

I may look on the relationship between the sexes in the Old Testament as pretty neanderthal, but judging from the response to the 'Me Too', things have not changed that much in the interim.

28th Sunday of the Year (B) 2018

'Jesus .... said to him. Go, sell what you have, and give to the poor and you will have treasure in heaven; then come, follow me.'

Jesus invited (called) this man to be one of his Apostles. This calling required that he abandon all his worldly attachments and possessions. This was for him 'a bridge too far.'

Although I am not invited to be an Apostle, I am nevertheless invited by my God to share the assets God has gifted to me with those in need.

The Governments of the world seem to be determined to accumulate the gifts God has given us in as few hands as possible. We are now in a situation where many people in work no longer earn a living wage. Where it can take a lifetime to acquire ones own home even when both husband and wife are working full-time. Where 'our' governments are no longer 'our' governments but the government of the wealthiest five or ten percent. Where truth is no longer available and news is a hodgepodge of fiction and spin. Where war and civil strife are waged (by proxy) by financial interests and multinational companies to gain control of the natural resources of poor countries; totally ignoring the welfare of these countries' populations.

There is little you and I can do politically to remedy this situation as successive governments seem to fall prey to the same vested interests.

What we can do is share our good fortune with those in need, by supporting the appropriate charities where we know that our donations go to the needy and not to the inflated salaries and expense accounts of fat cat 'CEOs' and directors. The smaller the charity the more likely it is to deserve our support and to use it effectively.

Anyone who gives regularly and generously will have experienced the joy it brings and the freedom it gives from attachment to money and possessions.

29th Sunday of the Year (B) 2018

We are so used to people blowing their own trumpet that we take it for granted.

We should be aware that self-praise is no praise. It amazes me how often I listen closely to someone telling me about all they do and have achieved, and more or less believing it. Even we can recommend a person for a job or a position solely on the strength at what that person has said about themselves. We make an art of self-promotion and self-deception.

When I feel the need to praise myself or the amount of work I do or to emphasise how busy I am, it is because I am unsure of myself or of my abilities. Self-praise demonstrates my weakness rather than my strengths.

Today's Gospel reading is alien to the mores of this world.

It emphasises the gulf which exists between life in the Kingdom of God and our everyday life and aspirations. And I quote "You know that those who are recognised as rulers over the Gentiles lord it over them, and their great ones make their authority over them felt. But it shall not be so among you. Rather, whoever wishes to be great among you will be your servant; whoever wishes to be first among you will be the slave of all. For the Son of Man did not come to be served but to serve and to give his life as a ransom for many."

It surprises me that so many of you here in our parish do spend so much time and energy in service to others. Your example helps me, and I am sure many others, to do a reality check on our own commitment to service to others.

The seats at the high table in the Kingdom of God will not be allocated to the dignitaries of State, Church or commerce but to those whose lives have been ones of humble service.

30th Sunday of the Year (B) 2018

Life is a bit like a batsman in cricket. Balls come at you fast, slow or in between. They spin and bounce this way or that way. They can bounce short or long etc. No matter how good you are you are eventually bowled out.

When bowled out the batsman does not give up playing the game. He/She learns from the experience and continues to try and improve their game.

Many Christians, when they are bowled out give up the game. They experience their faith and trust in God wavering and fading when they experience difficulties in life. They ask angrily 'why me?

They are annoyed at God and ask 'what good is God to me?' What do I get out of it?' Today's Gospel reading shows us Bartimaeus. Imagine him a strong resourceful man earning a good living. He goes blind. He cannot work any more. He becomes a huge burden on his wife and family. He is led to the side of a road every day by one of his children to beg from passers bye in an effort to eke out some sort of a living. His and his families' once strong religious observance now seems pointless. They do not attend the Synagogue any more except rarely.

But there is still something there - a faint spark of faith and hope in the God of his earlier life.

Hearing from the unusual crowd that Jesus of Nazareth, the so called 'prophet,' the so called 'man of God' is passing by, Bartimaeus, in his despair and depression at what life has thrown at him, cries out in a last gasp of fading faith and hope - "Jesus, Son of David, have mercy on me."

A lot of us find ourselves or have at one time found ourselves in a spiritual position like Bartimaeus. Our faith and hope in God is formless, wispy, inconsequential, unhelpful, pointless. I am almost fully convinced that there is nothing there for me.

This is the time, in my spiritual blindness, in my spiritual helplessness, in my spiritual barrenness, in my rapidly fading faith and hope, to cry out "Jesus, Son of David, have mercy on me."

32ND SUNDAY OF THE YEAR (B) 2018

We remember today and pray for all those who lost their lives as a result of the First World War.

It is good to remember and contemplate the enormity of what happened.

Casualties are estimated at 9 million combatants, 7 million civilians, between 50 and 100 million who succumbed to the flu epidemic which began towards the end of the war and to which the war was a major contributing factor.

While attending a local C of E church at an ecumenical service I noticed a plaque on the wall naming those from the village who had lost their lives in the war. The number was either 7 or 9 (I can't quite remember now as it was 17 or 18 years ago.) Even today the village is a small place. Imagine that in 1914 it was a very small huddle of houses centered around their church. Everyone knew each other intimately. The inhabitants would have either worked underground in the stone quarries or on the local large estate.

Imagine the grief and shock in that hamlet at the loss of what was probably most if not all their young men.

Multiply this anguish and loss, millions and millions of times over, in families, hamlets, villages and towns all over the world.

And has the human race learned anything from this great tsunami of grief and loss and despair? We have learned how to slaughter each other in far greater numbers and far more efficiently.

This is what we call Original sin. This is the name Christianity gives to our propensity to bring harm and grief on ourselves and on each other.

That is why we need salvation. That is why we need a new heaven and a new earth. As we read in 2 Peter; 'We await new heavens and a new earth in which righteousness dwells.'

We pray and hope that all the victims of World War 1 are now experiencing this new heaven and new earth.

33rd Sunday of the Year (B) 2018

I am not in favour of every Thomas, Richard and Harold picking up the Bible and reading it without adequate preparation, direction and guidance.

You take today's three readings. Can any one of you explain them to me? Did they mean anything to you? What meaning did you get from any one of the readings and if you got any meaning was it what the author intended?

I know you have, over the years, been told and urged to read the Bible.

By and large reading the Bible without knowing a fair bit about it and especially about the particular book you are reading can often lead to confusion. After all the thousands of different Christian Churches differ in their understanding of the Bible at least to some extent.

You take today's first reading from the Book of Daniel. Daniel was a fictional character. Whoever the author was, lived about 160 BC and wrote in symbolic prophetic language about events that had already happened.

The second reading from Hebrews although attributed to Paul is very likely not written by him. It was written about 60 - 69 AD. It seeks to convince the Jewish Christians of that time that the one sacrifice of Jesus of Nazareth on the Cross superseded and abrogated the many and differing sacrifices of the Temple in Jerusalem - of the Old Testament.

FATHER JOHN

The Gospel reading is a hotchpotch of apocalyptic accounts about the end of the world, about the destruction of Jerusalem in 70 AD. and about one's own death, all mixed up together.

Why did our church put on these three readings today? As you say if you are asked a question on the TV, the answer to which you do not know - you say; 'now that is a very good question.'

It is probably because we are approaching the end of the Liturgical year of the Church (in two weeks time) and they want me to sit up, review my relationship with my God and put my spiritual life in order.

Having said all this we must recognise that parts of the New Testament, especially the Gospels, are readily understandable and helpful to the most casual of readers. Many of the parables and instructions as regards how to live our daily lives are self evident and can be read over and over again and meditated on to ones advantage.

Feast of Christ the King (B) 2018

Human beings seem have three differing relationships with God; They ignore God. They fear God (Old Testament relationship). Or they have a New Testament relationship of gratitude, loyalty and love.

Old Testament relationship; Psalm 2. 'Serve the Lord with fear; with trembling bow down in homage, Lest God be angry and you perish from the way in a sudden blaze of anger.'

This is the attitude most of us were brought up to have with God.

Our Christianity was an unhappy religion made up of duties and obligations to be fulfilled. Our relationship with God was that of servant to master - a strict, demanding, accountant type of master. We had to earn, merit, achieve, win God's forgiveness, favour and salvation. Our religion was made up of rituals, liturgies, precepts, fixed prayers and times of prayers etc. - often only vaguely understood.

'Getting into heaven' was one's goal in life. This goal or prize was elusive, hard to attain and in constant danger of being lost due to our perceived sinfulness and the constant danger of falling prey to a multitude of 'mortal sins.'

All of us, bishops, priests and laity laboured and groaned under this burden. No wonder that joy, happiness and gratitude were so often absent in religion.

New Testament relationship: Eph. 2; 'For by grace you have been saved through faith, and this is not from you; it is the gift of God; it is not from works, so no one may boast.'

1 John 4: 'In this is love: not that we have loved God, but that he loved us (first) and sent his Son as expiation for our sins. Beloved, if God so loved us, we also must love one another.'

There is no fear in love, but perfect love drives out fear because fear has to do with punishment, and so one who fears is not yet perfect in love. Let us love, then, because God first loved us.'

Grace means a gratuitous, free gift from God which can in no way be merited or earned or achieved. Salvation is grace, freely offered. This free gift can be accepted or rejected.

It is good manners to feel and express gratitude for a gift. Religion is this normal response of gratitude to God the giver of the gift.

Various cultures and peoples have, over the centuries, developed different ways and means of showing their gratitude to God for this gift. But a true, valid response will always be solidly based on gratitude, appreciation and respect for the giver of the gift - God. You can call this love.

As every right-minded parent hopes for from their child, so too does God hope for gratitude, respect and love from His/Her children. How the child treats its parents, how I treat my God, will reveal the sort of person I am.

Since I came here I have had one ambition. To change my own and your attitude to God. It annoys me; It angers me to see and hear people treating God, my God, as a despotic, cruel, vengeful, selfish, small minded person.

Wake up. Look around you. Did you decide to be born? Did you give yourself the gift of life. Did you choose your gender, your colour, your height, what you look like, your intelligence etc?

All these were given to you. All these are gifts.

Of course you can accept a gift with gratitude and delight or you can accept it grudgingly and be unhappy and discontented. You can also reject the gift and kill yourself.

My attitude to God, my understanding of what my God is like, will affect my whole life. Am I worried about what God thinks of me? Am I fearful of what God might have in store for me? Do I worry as to whether I have sinned or not, whether I have fulfilled an obligation or not? Am I distressed about past faults? Am I forgiven or not? Have I done things the right way? This is a spiritual illness called scruples.

So let your attitude be one of boundless trust and confidence in God.

So forget about the past. Put the future in God's hands. Wake up every morning with joy in your heart for God is always with you - Immanuel.

'You have been told, 0 man, what is good, and what the Lord requires of you: Only to do right and to love goodness, and to walk humbly with your God.'

You have been saved. You are already a resident of the Kingdom of God. Act and speak in accordance with this fact. 'For God does not withdraw his mercy, nor permit even one of his promises to fail.'

www.ingramcontent.com/pod-product-compliance
Lightning Source LLC
Chambersburg PA
CBHW032102090426
42743CB00007B/207